C000054442

Public Opinion

Political Sociology series

Public Opinion

David L. Weakliem

polity

Copyright © David L. Weakliem 2020

The right of David L. Weakliem to be identified as Author of this Work has been asserted in accordance with the UK Copyright, Designs and Patents Act 1988.

First published in 2020 by Polity Press

Polity Press
65 Bridge Street
Cambridge CB2 1UR, UK

Polity Press
101 Station Landing
Suite 300
Medford, MA 02155, USA

All rights reserved. Except for the quotation of short passages for the purpose of criticism and review, no part of this publication may be reproduced, stored in a retrieval system or transmitted, in any form or by any means, electronic, mechanical, photocopying, recording or otherwise, without the prior permission of the publisher.

ISBN-13: 978-1-5095-2946-9
ISBN-13: 978-1-5095-2947-6(pb)

A catalogue record for this book is available from the British Library.

Library of Congress Cataloging-in-Publication Data
Names: Weakliem, David L., author.
Title: Public opinion / David L. Weakliem.
Description: Cambridge, UK ; Medford, MA : Polity Press, 2020. | Series:
    Political sociology series | Includes bibliographical references and
    index. | Summary: "Why your opinions are not necessarily your own"--
    Provided by publisher.
Identifiers: LCCN 2020000114 (print) | LCCN 2020000115 (ebook) |
    ISBN 9781509529469 (hardback) | ISBN 9781509529476 (paperback) |
    ISBN 9781509529490 (epub)
Subjects: LCSH: Public opinion.
Classification: LCC HM1236 .W43 2020 (print) | LCC HM1236 (ebook) | DDC
    303.3/8--dc23
LC record available at https://lccn.loc.gov/2020000114
LC ebook record available at https://lccn.loc.gov/2020000115

Typeset in 11 on 13 pt Sabon by
Servis Filmsetting Ltd, Stockport, Cheshire
Printed and bound in Great Britain by TJ International Limited

The publisher has used its best endeavours to ensure that the URLs for external websites referred to in this book are correct and active at the time of going to press. However, the publisher has no responsibility for the websites and can make no guarantee that a site will remain live or that the content is or will remain appropriate.

Every effort has been made to trace all copyright holders, but if any have been overlooked the publisher will be pleased to include any necessary credits in any subsequent reprint or edition.

For further information on Polity, visit our website: politybooks.com

Contents

Figures

In memory of Margaret F. Weakliem (1928–2017)

Acknowledgments

In a sense, this book began when I was a fellow at the Center for Advanced Study in the Behavioral Sciences in 1996–7. During that year, I began to think seriously about public opinion and explore some of the issues discussed in this book. I thank the Center for providing an excellent setting for research and reflection.

I also thank the students in my class in Public Opinion and Mass Communication at the University of Connecticut, who listened to me work out my ideas. I especially thank the students in the Fall 2019 class who gave me comments on drafts of chapters.

At Polity Press, Jonathan Skerrett suggested that I write a book on this topic and provided useful suggestions on how to approach it. Karina Jákupsdóttir encouraged me to keep going, even as I repeatedly fell behind schedule. Finally, six reviewers provided excellent comments on the manuscript.

I have drawn heavily on the collections of the Roper Center for Public Opinion Research. Unless otherwise indicated, survey questions mentioned in this book were obtained from the Roper Center's iPoll database. I also made use of SDA (Survey Documentation and Analysis) for analyses using the General Social Survey and American National Election Studies, and the World Values Survey website for analyses using the WVS.

Finally, I thank my wife Judith Milardo and stepdaughter Laura Spalding for putting up with many distracted silences while I worked on this book.

1

What is Public Opinion?

It seems obvious that in a democracy, the government should be guided by public opinion: after all, democracy means rule by the people. It is difficult, however, to say exactly what public opinion is: "to speak with precision of public opinion is a task not unlike coming to grips with the Holy Ghost" (Key 1961, p. 8). There are polls and surveys on many different topics, but these attempts to measure public opinion raise a number of questions. One is simple accuracy: can a survey given to 1,000 people tell us about the opinions of the whole nation? Others involve the interpretation of answers. Sometimes different surveys seem to point to different conclusions. In other cases, the results seem clear, but the underlying issues are complicated ones about which most people are not well informed. For example, recent surveys in the United States show widespread support for raising the minimum wage to $15.00 an hour, but many economists think that this would lead to a substantial increase in unemployment, which people presumably do not want. Suppose that these economists are correct: should we then conclude that the public does not really favor an increase, because it does not understand what effects it would have? Or should we say that the public thinks that an increase in the wages of low-wage workers is more important than any effect on employment, or that it favors some increase in the minimum wage, but is not committed to an exact number?

This chapter will address questions of measuring and interpreting public opinion. Subsequent chapters consider the relations between society and public opinion. There are often differences of average opinion among groups, such as social classes, racial and ethnic groups, or residents of cities and rural areas. Chapter 2 considers the reasons that such differences appear, persist, and change. Chapter 3 discusses the organization of opinions, particularly the distinction between left and right (liberal and conservative). Chapters 4 and 5 consider change in opinions: Chapter 4 focuses on the period for which survey data are available – from the 1930s to the present – while Chapter 5 takes a longer view and asks whether there are trends that extend over centuries. Finally, Chapter 6 considers how public attitudes toward government are changing, and what these changes mean for the future of democracy.

The Rise of Public Opinion

The expression "public opinion" first appeared in the late 1700s, and soon came into wide use. During the nineteenth century, many observers spoke of the power of public opinion. In 1823, Lord John Russell, a Member of Parliament and future Prime Minister of Great Britain, wrote: "it is the fashion to point out the increased and increasing influence of public opinion" (Russell 1823, p. 429). A few years later, a popular American college textbook called public opinion "the sense and sentiment of the community, necessarily irresistible, showing its sovereign power everywhere" (Lieber 1839, p. 253). At about the same time, Alexis de Tocqueville (1850 [1969], p. 124) wrote that public opinion was the "directing power" in both the United States and France, despite the differences in their forms of government: "in America it works through elections and decrees, in France by revolutions."

The appearance and growth of "public opinion" resulted from a change in the relationship between government and society. Plamenatz (1975, p. 345) defines public opinion as "opinions about the government and its policies current in circles outside the [government] hierarchy and yet close enough to it to acquire such opinions and to bring them to bear on it." For most of history, only a small elite group could regularly participate in government; most people had no way to even become aware of what policies or actions the government was considering. Ordinary people sometimes tried to influence the government through collective protests, but these usually involved objections to the conduct of local officials or landowners rather than attempts to change government policy (Tilly 1983). This situation started to change with the Industrial Revolution, as more people became aware of the government and acquired more means to influence it. The sources of this change included the spread of literacy, the appearance of newspapers and magazines, the growth of cities, and the expansion of the "middle class" – people with enough knowledge and leisure time to pay attention to public affairs. These developments meant that news could spread more quickly and be discussed more widely, so that people could form opinions about government policy and organize to influence it.

At first, public opinion was often understood to mean middle-class opinion, but the range of the "public" expanded as time went on. The weakening of property restrictions on voting and the general adoption of the secret ballot in the late nineteenth century were important parts of this process, since voting gave ordinary people an easy and inexpensive way to influence the government (Rokkan 1961). At the same time, rising educational levels and the growth of the mass media made it easier for people to be informed about public affairs. Today, the "public" is generally understood to include the entire adult population, and people have become accustomed to offering opinions on all kinds of topics.

Although nineteenth-century observers agreed that public opinion was important, they found it difficult be sure of what that opinion was on any given question. In an election, voters merely choose a party or a person: they do not get to vote on specific policy proposals. Moreover, candidates often give different messages to different audiences or use ambiguous language that can be interpreted in a variety of ways. As a result, we know that voters preferred *something* about the winner, but do not know exactly what that was. People can express opinions more precisely by letters and petitions to government officials, or by public rallies and demonstrations, but only a small fraction of the public engages in such actions, and it is possible that the opinions of the people who do not are very different from the opinions of those who do. Moreover, the opinions of the people who do not participate cannot safely be ignored: they might resist a policy after it is enacted or vote against the government at the next election. The positions taken by organizations and the opinions expressed in the media can also be taken as indicators of public opinion, but these have a similar limitation: the members of an organization might not share the views of the leaders, and the readers of a publication might not share the views of the writers.

Public Opinion Surveys

In the 1930s, a new form of measurement appeared which transformed the study of public opinion: the survey. The basic procedure of an opinion survey is to ask a standard set of questions to a group of people who are supposed to represent the public (the "sample"). Surveys are conducted in the same way that elections are: participants (also known as "respondents") answer the questions in private and are assured that their individual answers will not be disclosed. Interviewers are instructed to be neutral – to simply record answers without raising objections or expressing their own opinions. Usually the participants choose their answer from a standard list, rather than responding in their own words. In effect, every survey question can be regarded as a small-scale referendum conducted by secret ballot. George Gallup, who founded the first survey organization, saw surveys as a way to improve the operation of democracy by giving political leaders a more accurate and detailed picture of public opinion (Gallup 1938).

In addition to giving information on opinions in the public as a whole, surveys can include background questions on characteristics such as race, gender, and educational level, making it possible to distinguish the opinions of different kinds of people. Moreover, most surveys ask for opinions on a number of topics, so it is also possible to examine the relationships among different opinions, or between opinions and voting choices.

The first surveys were conducted by commercial organizations and focused on predicting elections and measuring opinion on issues of the day (surveys of this kind are often known as "polls"). If an issue remained prominent, the polls sometimes repeated questions that they had previously used. For example, the Gallup Poll asked "are you in favor of labor unions?" in July 1936, and asked the same question again in 1937, twice in 1938, three times in 1939, and twice in 1940. When questions are repeated, it is possible to examine changes in opinion, both in the general public and in specific groups. For example, in June 1937, 70 percent said that they were in favor of labor unions and 22 percent that they were not; in October 1938, 58 percent were in favor and 28 percent were not.

Academic researchers soon began to conduct surveys, and sometimes made systematic efforts to repeat questions on a regular basis. The American National Election Studies, which began in 1948, focused on voting and political opinions, while the General Social Survey began in 1972 and covered a wide range of topics. At the same time, other polls and surveys continue to repeat questions more or less frequently. As a result, there is now a record of change in public opinion, which on some topics extends over a period of more than eighty years.

Surveys were soon adopted in several other nations, including Canada, France, Australia, and Great Britain. National survey organizations sometimes agreed to include the same question, or sometimes several questions, in their polls, making it possible to compare opinion across nations. Academic researchers followed with more systematic efforts to develop "comparative surveys," in which an entire survey was translated into the local language and administered in different nations. Because of the expense and organizational effort necessary to carry out comparative surveys, only a few were conducted until the 1970s. Since that time, however, they have become more common, and some of them are part of continuing series that repeat questions over time. The Eurobarometer, which began in 1974, includes nations in the European Union. The World Values Survey began in 1981, when it included ten nations; the seventh wave, conducted in 2017–2020, will include about eighty nations from all parts of the world. Since 1985, the International Social Survey Programme has conducted an annual survey focusing on a particular topic: examples include the role of government in 2016, social networks in 2017, and religion in 2018.

The accumulation of survey data has increased the range of research that is possible: analysts are able to compare not only different kinds of people, but also different places or times, or all of these levels at once. For example, Brooks, Nieuwbeerta, and Manza (2006) used data from 112 election surveys to compare the effects of gender, class, and religion on voting choices in six nations between 1964 and 1998.

Another important recent development has been the increased use of survey experiments, in which different respondents in a survey are randomly selected to receive different information or different forms of a question. Simple experiments have been used since the beginnings of survey research but when surveys are given over the internet, it is possible to have more complex designs and use a wide variety of cues – for example, asking respondents to read a passage or watch a video before they answer a question.

Accuracy of Opinion Surveys

Sampling

A basic problem in survey research is how to obtain a representative sample – a sample that is like the population in all respects, except that it includes a smaller number of people. At first, most surveys sought to achieve this goal by "quota samples." In this method, interviewers were given quotas for certain characteristics that were thought be important for opinion, such as gender, race, and age, and were otherwise left free to choose respondents in any way they saw fit. For example, an interviewer might be instructed to obtain twenty interviews, which would include ten men and ten women, seventeen whites and three blacks, four people aged 18 to 29, twelve people aged 30 to 64, and four people aged 65 and above (see Berinsky 2006 for a more detailed description of the procedures used in early surveys). Although this method guaranteed the sample would be representative in terms of the characteristics for which there were quotas, it did not necessarily make it representative in other respects. For example, if interviewers obtained their samples by approaching people in public places, then people who rarely left their homes or who worked unusual hours would be underrepresented.

An alternative way of obtaining a representative sample is a random (probability) sample, in which every person is assigned a definite chance of being chosen for the sample, and the decision of whether to include them is made at random – in effect, by a lottery. There is no guarantee that a particular random sample will be exactly representative, but it is likely to be close to the population. Suppose that a random sample of 1,000 people is drawn from a population in which 50 percent are women. It is likely (about an 80% chance) that between 48 and 52 percent of the people in the sample will be women, and almost certain (about a 99.9% chance) that between 45 and 55 percent will be women.

Random samples have three major advantages over quota samples. The first is that they will be approximately representative in terms of *all* characteristics, not just the ones that are included in the quotas. The second is that as a random sample becomes larger, the distribution of characteristics in the sample tends to come closer to the distribution in the population. This means that the accuracy of the sample estimates can be increased by increasing the size of the sample. For example, suppose that the population is 50 percent female. The chance that the sample will be within two percent of that figure – that is, between 48 and 52 percent female – rises from about 80 percent in a random sample of 1,000 to about 97 percent in a sample of 3,000 and 99.5 percent in a sample of 5,000. In contrast, with other methods of sampling, increasing the size of the sample will not necessarily bring it closer to the population. The third advantage of a random sample is related to the second: given the size of the sample, it is possible to calculate a "margin of error" – that is, to estimate how much difference there might be between the sample and the population.

In the United States, most surveys shifted from quota samples to random samples after about 1950. This change was facilitated by the growth of telephone ownership, which made it easier to obtain a random sample. If everyone has a telephone, then a random sample of the public can be obtained by simply dialing randomly generated telephone numbers. Quota sampling lasted longer in many other countries, but random sampling has come to be the standard method. Experience shows that quota sampling often was reasonably effective, and statistical adjustments can be applied to produce a closer match to a representative sample (Berinsky, Powell, Shickler, and Yohai 2011). Nevertheless, random sampling is preferred because it has a firm theoretical foundation – we know that a random sample is likely to be accurate within limits determined by the size of the sample.

Non-Response

In principle, random sampling provides a definitive solution to the problem of choosing a representative sample. In practice, however, researchers do not have complete control over the sample. Survey researchers can attempt to contact a random sample of the public, but some of the people in that sample will not be at home, and others will refuse to participate. If the people who do not participate are different from those who do – for example, more suspicious or less interested in public affairs – then the people who actually answer the questions will not be a representative sample of the population. The proportion of people who do not respond has been increasing in recent decades, partly because it has become easier for people to screen telephone calls, and partly because people have simply become more reluctant to participate in surveys. Obtaining high response rates is still possible – the response rate to the 2016 General Social Survey was over 60 percent – but it is time consuming and expensive. Typical telephone surveys today have response rates of less than ten percent (Keeter et al. 2017).

Unlike sampling error, the error resulting from non-response will not become smaller as the sample size increases.

Is Accuracy Declining?

The rising rates of non-response have led to concerns that surveys are becoming less accurate. The results of the British referendum on membership in the European Union in June 2016 and the American presidential election in November 2016 surprised many observers and led to a good deal of criticism of the polls. However, closer examination shows that the polls were not far off in either case. In the referendum, they indicated that the vote would be close: the average who said that they would vote to remain was 51 percent in the final polls before the EU referendum (Hanretty 2016). Moreover, the margin seemed to narrow as the referendum approached, and several polls taken in the month before the vote showed a majority in favor of leaving (Hobolt 2016, p. 1262). Because the race was close, a relatively small error in the polls was enough to make a difference in the outcome of the referendum. In the United States, the average of surveys taken just before the election showed Hillary Clinton with 46.8 percent of the vote and Donald Trump with 43.6 percent (RealClear Politics 2016). In fact, Clinton received 48.2 percent and Trump received 46.2 percent. That is, Clinton's lead in the vote was 2.0 percent, only slightly smaller than the 3.2 percent average of the surveys. A review by the American Association for Public Opinion Research (AAPOR 2017) concluded that the national polls were somewhat *more* accurate in 2016 than in most recent elections, although some of the state polls were less accurate.

A comprehensive study by Jennings and Wlezien (2018) including elections from 45 nations over 75 years found no evidence that survey predictions are becoming less accurate. However, the decline in response rates means that "random" samples now are in much the same position as quota samples: they seem to represent the population fairly well in practice, but there is no guarantee that they will continue to do so. Some survey organizations have turned to selecting respondents from a pool of people who have agreed to participate in surveys, and then weighting the sample to match the population in terms of various characteristics. In a sense, this approach is a more sophisticated kind of quota sampling (see Hillygus 2016, pp. 39–43 for further discussion).

The comparison of election results to survey predictions offers some general lessons for the interpretation of surveys. First, the people who do not respond are generally less interested and less engaged than those who do. Surveys regularly over-estimate voter turnout, and it is reasonable to assume that they also over-estimate general levels of political knowledge and interest. They may also over-estimate confidence in social institutions and under-estimate levels of alienation and general discontent. Second, there is some unpredictable variation in survey results beyond what could be expected from sampling error. Given the number of surveys taken before American presidential elections, the expected sampling error in the average of all predictions is very small, less than one tenth of one percent. However, there is often a difference of about two or three percent between the average survey prediction and the actual results (Traugott 2005). For example, if an average of all polls shows a candidate getting 52 percent of the vote, it would not be too unusual for that candidate to lose narrowly, or to get 54 or 55 percent of the vote. This error does not have any consistent direction – sometimes the Democrats do better than predicted, and sometimes the Republicans do (AAPOR 2017, p. 11). The general implication is that when considering the possibility of change in public opinion, we should focus on large or sustained movements – small differences from year to year could be illusory, even if they are statistically significant.

The Effects of Public Opinion

Even if a sample accurately represents the population, the survey is an unusual kind of interaction – an anonymous interview with a stranger, in which people are not challenged or asked to explain or justify their opinions. Do the opinions expressed in this special situation correspond to what people would do or say in other settings?

Although experience shows that surveys are useful in predicting elections, surveys are designed on the model of an election, where a person casts a vote in private. This point raises a question of whether the opinions measured in surveys can predict other kinds of behavior. The noted historian Arthur M. Schlesinger, Jr. maintained that the kind of public opinion measured in surveys is of little interest: "public opinion polling . . . elicits essentially an irresponsible expression of opinion – irresponsible because no action is intended to follow the expression . . . it is responsible opinion – opinion when the chips are down, opinion which issues directly in decision and action – which is relevant to the historical process and of primary interest to the historian" (Schlesinger 1962). That is, opinions which do not lead to action do not affect history.

However, since Schlesinger wrote, there has been a good deal of research on the relationship between public opinion and government policy, and the conclusion is that the opinions measured in surveys do have an influence. Erikson, MacKuen, and Stimson (2002) and Soroka and Wlezien (2010) examine changes in public opinion and government policies over time and find that when public opinion moves in one direction, policy generally follows it. This connection holds even after taking account of the party in power: for example, when American public opinion became more conservative in the late 1970s, policies did as well, although there was a Democratic president and Democratic majorities in both houses of Congress. Gilens (2012) compares proposed laws, and finds that those which get more support in surveys are more likely to be enacted, although he also finds that the opinions of affluent people have more influence than those of ordinary people. Borch (2007) compares states, and finds that those in which public opinion is more liberal tend to have more liberal policies. Brooks and Manza (2008) compare nations and find that public opinion predicts spending on social welfare programs, while Crutchfield and Pettinicchio (2009) find that nations with a higher "taste for inequality" have more income inequality and higher rates of imprisonment.

One possible reason that the opinions measured in surveys influence policy is that public officials pay attention to surveys, presumably because they believe that enacting popular policies will help them to win re-election. Another is that often the opinions expressed in surveys result in action, perhaps not the dramatic kind that Schlesinger spoke of, but in various kinds of everyday behavior. For example, attitudes toward other racial and ethnic groups can be expressed in interactions with neighbors, friends, and co-workers. If this is the case, public opinion may have a direct effect on social conditions, apart from government policy. Weakliem, Andersen, and Heath (2005) find that income inequality is higher in nations where more people say that more productive workers deserve to be paid more than their less productive colleagues. Their explanation is that employers have to pay attention to popular beliefs about fairness when setting wages. People have ways of communicating these ideas through behavior: for example, by working harder when they think they are being paid fairly or being more likely to quit when they think that they are not.

Nevertheless, Schlesinger makes an important point. What he calls "opinion which issues directly in decision and action" may not be the only kind that matters, but it is likely to have more effect than opinions which are expressed in private. Moreover, collective action is not just a spontaneous expression of opinion, but requires organization and resources. The implication is that social movements can have an independent influence on policy, apart from general public opinion. Nevertheless, a favorable climate of public opinion will help a movement to survive and grow, since it means that there are more potential supporters and fewer potential opponents. For their part, social movements often try to influence general public opinion.

Interpreting Survey Responses

Another concern about surveys is whether they can represent opinions on complex issues. Different questions that seem to have the same meaning sometimes produce substantially different responses. For example, in August 1953, when asked "as things stand now, do you feel that the war in Korea has been worth fighting, or not?" only 27 percent said that it had. A month later, another survey asked "As you look back on the Korean war, do you think the United States did the right thing in sending troops to stop the Communist invasion, or should we have stayed out of it entirely?": 64 percent said the United States did the right thing (Mueller 1973). There is no reason to think that opinions about the war changed dramatically during this time, so the apparent difference of opinion must have been due to the difference in the questions.

A contemporary example is provided by three recent survey questions on the death penalty. When asked "Would you like to see the death penalty abolished nationwide, or not" 31 percent said that it should be abolished. When asked, "Which punishment do you prefer for people convicted of murder? ... The death penalty, life in prison with no chance of parole," 47 percent chose the death penalty and 52 percent life without parole. Finally, when asked "In general, what do you think should be the punishment for people convicted of murder? Death penalty, life in prison with no chance of parole, depends on the circumstances," 80 percent chose the death penalty or "depends on the circumstances," and only 19 percent chose a life sentence without parole. The answers to the different questions suggest levels of support for the keeping the death penalty might be as low as 47 percent or as high as 80 percent.

Sometimes differences of this kind can be interpreted by supposing that some people have views that are too complex to be represented by either question alone. A person who agreed with the decision to send troops to Korea but disagreed with the subsequent conduct of the war might say the war had not been worth fighting; someone who believed that the death penalty is sometimes justified in principle but did not trust the criminal justice to apply it fairly might favor abolishing it. However, there are cases in which it is not possible to reconcile the answers to different questions in this way. For example, in December 2013 a survey asked "The federal minimum wage is now $7.25. Do you think the federal minimum wage should be raised, lowered, or should it remain the same?" 71

said that the minimum wage should be raised, 25 percent
should remain the same, and only two percent said that it
be lowered. In January 2014 another survey asked: "As
you may know, the federal government sets the national minimum
wage – the lowest rate in dollars per hour that most workers
should be paid – which is now set at seven dollars and twenty-five
cents an hour. Which of the following comes closest to your view
on how the federal government should handle the minimum wage?
. . . The government should raise the minimum wage because it
would help lots of people pay their bills. The government should
not raise the minimum wage because it would cause businesses
to cut jobs. There shouldn't be a minimum wage because government shouldn't tell businesses what to pay their employees." In
response to this question, 56 percent were in favor of an increase,
25 percent said it should stay the same, and 15 percent said there
should not be a minimum wage. That is, one survey found that
only two percent thought that the minimum wage should be less
than $7.25, while the other found that 15 percent thought that it
should be abolished completely. The only plausible explanation
for this difference is that some people were persuaded when they
heard the argument that "the government shouldn't tell businesses
what to pay their employees."

Sometimes the same question will get different responses depending on the questions that precede it in the survey. In one dramatic
example from the early 1970s, 37 percent said they were in favor
of allowing Soviet journalists in the United States, but when the
question followed one about whether the Soviet Union should
allow American journalists, 73 percent were in favor (Schuman
and Presser 1981).

Zaller (1992) proposed a model that helps to makes sense of
the effects of question wording and question order on responses.
In his view, even people who are well informed and interested in
public affairs do not have definite "positions" on most issues in
the way that a candidate for public office might. Rather, people
have a variety of relevant feelings, thoughts, and pieces of information. When they answer survey questions, people "make up
attitude reports as best they can as they go along," based on

the considerations that come to mind (Zaller 1992, p. 76). As a result, their answers are influenced by the information that they heard most recently, whether in the question itself or in previous questions. For example, mention of the "Communist invasion" suggests a reason to favor American involvement in the Korean War, and the last question on the minimum wage raises a point that might not otherwise have occurred to people. Even smaller differences in question wording can suggest different ways of thinking about the issue: for example, simply including a "depends on circumstances" option to a question on the death penalty draws attention to the possibility that it could be applied less often without being eliminated. Zaller's model suggests that the best picture of public opinion on a topic is obtained by looking at answers to a range of questions, rather than trying to identify some questions as fair and dismissing others as biased. If there are differences among the responses to different questions on the same topic, those differences tells us something about the arguments, information, or frames of reference that influence people's conclusions.

Change in Opinions

Bourdieu (1979) observes that when an issue becomes the focus of attention, changes in opinion will take place through social interaction, not just private reflection. For example, when workers are deciding whether to go on strike, they will hear arguments and appeals from co-workers, management, and their families and friends. Furthermore, if the strike takes place, their opinions are likely to change as a result of their experience. The way that people remember and interpret that experience will also depend on social interaction. The implication of his argument is that the opinions that people express in a survey may be very different from the those that subsequently develop: "opinion surveys capture quite well the structure of opinions at a given moment, but they do not capture the potential state of opinion, and more exactly, the movement of opinion" (Bourdieu 1979, p. 128).

Key (1961) made a similar point in proposing the idea of "latent opinion," by which he meant "opinion that might exist at some point in the future" (Zaller 2003, p. 311). He noted that, in order to be successful, politicians need to consider latent opinion – that is, to anticipate what opinion will be under some future conditions. For example, a candidate may suspect that a position which is popular now will become less popular when faced with arguments that opponents are likely to raise.

Bourdieu is correct in suggesting that surveys do not shed much light on the process of change in the opinions of individuals. In most cases, surveys taken before and after the event will include different people, so it is not even possible to identify the people who changed their opinion. Of course, it is possible to ask people if their opinions changed, but there is no way to know if those answers are accurate.It is possible to measure individual change by using "panel" surveys, which return to the same sample. However, although panel surveys can show whether a person's opinions have changed between the first and second time that a question is asked, they do not observe people at the moment that their opinions are changing. Moreover, someone who gives the same answer both times might have changed their mind in between before returning to their original opinion. Another important limitation is that when the sample contains only a small fraction of the population, as is usually the case, it is not possible to get much information about social interaction. For example, the people with whom a respondent discussed an issue are not likely to be included in the sample, so it is not possible to get direct measures of their opinions or other characteristics.

However, surveys can show the extent and nature of change in overall public opinion, as well as opinion in different groups. With any single comparison, such as the decline in support for labor unions between July 1937 and October 1938 mentioned earlier in this chapter, it is usually possible to think of a large number of factors that might have caused the change. However, when there are more occasions to compare, it may become possible to see patterns, in which certain kinds of events are generally followed by changes in public opinion. For example, there is a "rally round the flag" effect in which foreign crises are usually followed by an increase in support for the government (Baker and Oneal 2001). Persily (2008, pp. 11–12) suggests that Supreme Court decisions sometimes produce a "backlash" in the short run, but that over the long term public opinion gradually shifts in favor of them.

Other Ways of Measuring Public Opinion

Although surveys are now the major source of information on public opinion, there are some other methods that can be useful for certain purposes. One is in-depth interviews, in which respondents can answer in their own words and the interviewer has the freedom to draw them out, probe apparent inconsistencies, and go back to reconsider issues that were previously discussed. These interviews provide direct information about the process of thinking and the reasons that people have for their opinions. Furthermore, ambivalence, uncertainty, or idiosyncratic points of view are revealed more clearly than they would be in a conventional survey.

In-depth interviews share one of the limitations of standard surveys: they are a conversation between the interviewer and the subject, so they do not involve social interaction among peers. Focus groups try to model the process of social interaction by gathering a small group of people who discuss issues under the general guidance of a moderator. They make it possible to see how opinions develop and change in the course of discussion and how people respond to different arguments and counter-arguments. Focus groups are often used by political campaigns and market researchers, who are interested not only in learning about opinions, but in discovering how to influence opinions. For example, a focus group can be used to test possible themes for a campaign and decide which one would be most effective.

Although focus groups involve social interaction, it is interaction of a kind that does not normally occur in social life. Focus groups involve intensive discussion of some topic, and usually include people who are not previously acquainted with each other. Most discussion of political issues, in contrast, occurs among friends, family members, or acquaintances, and is usually brief and intermittent. People rarely explore a topic in depth, and there is no moderator to keep them from moving on to another topic. Public opinion can be investigated in a more natural setting by means of ethnographic research, in which a researcher spends time with people in the course of their daily lives.

Compared to surveys, all of these methods have the advantage of giving more direct information about the process by which opinions are formed. Consequently, they can shed light on the connection, or lack of connection, between opinions on different topics. With a survey, it is possible to measure a correlation between the answers to different questions, but the interpretation of the correlation must be provided by the researcher. With an in-depth interview or a focus group, the participants can offer their own account of how and why they see the issues as connected.

The alternatives to surveys have two important limitations. The first is that they must be based on small and unrepresentative samples. These methods generally require face-to-face contact, so samples must be limited to one location. They also demand a good deal of time and effort from the participants, so the people who agree to participate are almost certainly not representative of the general population. Finally, it is difficult to standardize the procedures, so the investigator cannot use assistants to gather information from a larger sample. The second limitation is that it is not possible to express their results in a standard form, or to be confident that another investigator who had studied a comparable group of people would have come to the same conclusions. With conventional surveys, in contrast, it is possible to check the results by asking the same questions to another random sample from the same population. In contrast, ethnographies, focus groups, and interviews are more idiosyncratic – two researchers examining the same topic might come to very different conclusions.

The strengths of surveys are that they can be based on reasonably representative samples and that they allow exact comparisons among places or times, or groups of people. Consequently, surveys are likely to remain the primary source of information about public opinion. The other methods are a useful supplement, however, especially in helping to interpret the results of surveys. Lazarsfeld (1944) proposed that "good research consists in weaving back and forth between [open-ended methods] and the more cut-and-dried procedures" of standard surveys.

Surveys also have an important practical limitation – they were developed only in the 1930s. Moreover, surveys necessarily ask about issues that seem important at the time, so they often neglect ones that later come to be seen as important. For example, there were only a handful of survey questions about attitudes toward gays and lesbians until the mid-1970s. There were no questions on important events such as the Stonewall riots and the American Psychiatric Association's decision to remove homosexuality from its official list of mental disorders. Sometimes the absence of survey questions can be telling. No survey organization seems to have asked about the internment of Japanese-Americans during the Second World War, or about reactions to the 1944 Supreme Court decision that found the internment to be constitutional, and this absence suggests that the policy was not regarded as particularly controversial at the time.

However, the entire history of survey research covers only about eighty years. As a result, discussions of the history of public opinion must either confine themselves to the recent past or use other sources to make inferences about public opinion. Newspapers and magazines provide some guidance: if an opinion is expressed frequently in publications with large circulation, it is reasonable to conclude that it was held by a substantial number of people. The tone of the articles – whether they treat their opinion as a matter of simple common sense or as a controversial position that needs to be explained and defended – also provides clues about the authors' judgment of public opinion.

Another source of information on public opinion is the reports of contemporary observers, which are based on some combination of reading, talking to people, and living in the society. Lipset (1962) observes that since the eighteenth century there have been many attempts to describe the climate of opinion in the United States, and that despite differences among the accounts, there are some common themes. Although the literature on America is particularly rich, there are similar reports for many other countries. Moreover, discussions of America by foreign observers often include explicit or explicit comparisons with public opinion in their own countries.

Although these kinds of historical records cannot provide precise information about the distribution of opinion, they allow for broad generalizations. For example, it seems safe to say that there was little support for women's suffrage in the middle of the nineteenth century, but that by the early twentieth century support and opposition were about equally matched, and that after the passage of the Nineteenth Amendment, opposition quickly faded away.

Public Opinion and Popular Opinion

To this point, the discussion has assumed that public opinion involves all of the people. Some observers, however, distinguish between public opinion and what Nisbet (1975) calls "popular opinion." In their view, public opinion is limited to a smaller group of people who are well informed, public spirited, or distinguished in some other way. This distinction could be understood as a normative one – a claim that the opinions of some people should be given more weight. However, it also has some empirical content, since it raises questions about the effect of different kinds of information and social interaction on opinions. An opinion might be based on accurate information, careful thought, and extensive discussion with a range of people, or on prejudice and superficial thought.

Some of these questions can be investigated using surveys: for example, it is possible to compare the opinions of more and less informed people, or to see whether people with different opinions react differently to new information. Others can be investigated using in-depth interviews or focus groups.

Sociology and Public Opinion

Finally, what is the role of sociology in the study of public opinion? The topic of public opinion is of interest to several disciplines, including psychology, political science, and communications, and is often discussed by journalists and the general public. Although there is a good deal of overlap between the perspectives of different disciplines, there are some differences of emphasis. Sociology is particularly concerned with what Lipset (1960) called the "social bases" of opinion. This phrase is sometimes understood to mean differences of opinion among groups such as social classes or ethnic groups, but it has a deeper meaning. The basic principle is that opinions are formed, maintained, and changed by social interaction. To a large extent, our opinions are adopted from the people around us, so any group in which interaction takes place is likely to develop some distinctive patterns of opinion. As Berelson, Lazarsfeld, and McPhee (1954, p. 311) observe, "political preferences may . . . be considered analogous to cultural tastes – in music, literature, recreational activities, dress, ethics, speech, social behavior." One implication of this principle is that any social change that affects patterns of interaction will produce a change in the distribution of opinions. This does not necessarily mean that public opinion "reflects" social conditions in a direct fashion: there are complex interactions involving existing opinions, political and social institutions, and social conditions. However, the principle means that sociology is ultimately concerned with the comparison of different societies rather than different individuals. The growth of cross-national and historical evidence discussed earlier in this chapter means that the potential to make these kinds of comparisons is growing rapidly.

Sociology had an important part in the early development of research on public opinion, but turned away from the topic in the 1960s and 1970s (Manza and Brooks 2012). More recently, some sociologists have returned to the field, and researchers from other disciplines have started to consider "sociological" perspectives. For example, the political scientists Achen and Bartels

(2016, pp. 213–31) argue that research on public opinion and voting should pay more attention to group identities. Moreover, several developments in society, including political polarization, controversies over "identity politics," and the rise of social media, have led to renewed interest in the ways that social interaction affects opinions. The premise of this book is that the study of public opinion can benefit from a sociological perspective, and that sociologists can benefit from thinking more systematically about public opinion.

Summary and Conclusions

This chapter began by discussing the rise of the idea of public opinion and its connection to the rise of democratic government. It then discussed the measurement of public opinion, especially through polls and surveys. Experience suggests that surveys provide reasonably accurate measures of public opinion, and that their accuracy has not been declining. However, surveys have some limitations as measures of public opinion, and there are other methods that can help to fill in the gaps. Finally, it discussed the distinctive contribution of sociology: the principle that opinions are formed through social interaction.

2

The Social Bases of Public Opinion

People form opinions in the course of everyday interactions with family, friends, neighbors, and workmates. This simple principle has far-reaching implications, which will be explored in this chapter.

The Formation of Group Differences

A basic principle of social interaction is that most people prefer to agree rather than to disagree, especially when they are talking with friends or family members. If someone offers an opinion in a group of friends, those who agree with that opinion are likely to speak up in support of it, while those who disagree are likely to remain silent or try to change the subject. As a result, only one point of view will be heard, so that members of the group who started without a clear opinion will be more likely to accept that point of view. If the topic comes up again, the people who support what seems to be the prevailing view will become more confident, and will speak more freely. Those who do not support it will be in an uncomfortable position: they must either remain silent or speak up in opposition to their friends. They may resolve the conflict by gradually suppressing their doubts and coming to accept the majority view.

Therefore, the result of social interaction is a tendency toward "political homogeneity" (Berelson, Lazarsfeld, and McPhee 1954,

p. 116): the distribution of opinion in a group of people who communicate with each other will be more one-sided than it would have been if the individual members of the group had independently come to their own conclusions. Huckfeldt and Sprague (1988) speak of the "informational coercion of minorities": this does not necessarily mean that minorities experience explicit pressure to conform, but that it is more difficult for them to find support for their views, so they are more likely to abandon them.

The process of interaction in face-to-face groups has implications for larger groups such as social classes or adherents of a religion. People usually associate with people who are similar to themselves, a tendency known as "homophily" (McPherson, Smith-Lovin, and Cook 2001). That is, friends, family members, and co-workers tend to be similar in terms of social class, ethnicity, religion, and other characteristics. If the tendency toward homophily is strong, the great majority of a person's associates will be from the same group, and so will the associates of those associates. As a result, even opinions and information that a person hears at second or third-hand will be primarily from other members of the group. Consequently, the same pressure toward homogeneity that applies in a face-to-face group will also apply in the larger group. In contrast, if homophily is weak, people will encounter more views from outside their group, so that the tendency toward homogeneity will be weaker.

The same general social processes are relevant to all kinds of tastes and opinions – for example, musical tastes or preferences for different consumer goods – but there are two special features that apply to political opinions. One is the importance of political parties and leaders. The competitive aspect of election campaigns provides a continuing stream of new material for conversation and encourages people to take sides, so popular discussion of politics often focuses on personalities and electoral performance rather than issues. Consequently, people are likely to develop a stronger commitment to parties or political figures than to specific opinions: if a party changes its position on an issue, supporters of that party often change their opinions rather than reconsider their support for the party (Achen and Bartels 2016, pp. 258–64; Lenz 2013).

A second feature is that political opinions are influenced by feelings about other groups. In choosing entertainment or consumer goods, people who have different preferences can simply go their own ways. Politics, in contrast, necessarily involves collective decisions that affect other people. Therefore, people will tend to favor policies that help groups about which they have positive feelings, and oppose policies that help groups about which they have negative feelings. These two features of political opinions are connected, because support for a party is often based on a general sense that it cares about certain kinds of people, rather than on agreement with specific policy positions.

Factors Affecting Group Differences

People can be classified in many different ways – for example, by age, marital status, parenthood, occupation, health, whether they rent or own their home – but only a few of these qualities are consistently related to opinions on public affairs. What distinguishes them from others? One factor, as already suggested, is the degree of homophily associated with the group. If people who share some quality have little contact with each other, there will be no pressure for homogeneity of opinions. A second is the usual duration of membership – the longer people tend to stay in a group, the more likely that the group will become part of their fundamental identity. A third is the degree to which membership is passed on from generation to generation. If membership in a group is inherited, then its impact will begin in childhood, when people are most open to influence. Putting these points together, the groups that can be expected to have most influence on opinion are those which have a high degree of homophily, are stable over a person's lifetime, and for which membership is passed on from one generation to the next. Berelson, Lazarsfeld, and McPhee (1954) proposed that these conditions applied most strongly to ethnicity and race, religion, geographical location, and social class.

Homophily may be very high for ethnicity: in many cases, a person's friends and family members are almost entirely from their own group. Ethnic differences sometimes correspond to linguistic differences, which makes the tendency for homophily even stronger. Ethnicity also remains the same over a person's life and is transmitted across generations. As a result, racial and ethnic differences in opinion can be very large and enduring.

Religion is usually less immediately visible than ethnic origin. Consequently, although the tendency toward religious homophily is often strong, interaction is more likely to take place across religious boundaries than across ethnic boundaries. Religion has a good deal of continuity across the lifespan and between generations, but is not completely fixed: people can convert to another religion or become more or less active in the practice of their religion. Consequently, religious differences in opinion are often substantial, but generally not as large as ethnic differences.

The tendency for homophily is fairly strong for social class: many social contacts are made at work, and friends and neighbors are usually of approximately the same economic level. Social class also has a good deal of continuity over adult life: a person who is a manual worker at age thirty is likely to remain a manual worker for the rest of his or her working life. However, although class has some continuity across the generations, there is also a good deal of social mobility – upward or downward movement. Many people grew up in a different class position than the one they currently occupy, so the prevailing opinions they encountered when they were growing up may be different from the prevailing opinions in their contemporary environment. Another result of social mobility is that members of the same family may be in different social classes – for example, a professional might have a sibling who is a manual worker. As a result, many people have some contact with and concern for people who are members of other classes. These contacts can be expected to reduce class differences in opinion.

Finally, the place in which one lives is a strong influence on patterns of interaction. Although advances in technology have made it easier to keep in touch with people who live far away, communication is still more frequent among people who live near each other. Place of residence usually has a good deal of continuity over the lifetime and across generations. For example, in the United States, about two-thirds of people live in the state where they were born, and about 80 percent live in the same region (Molloy, Smith, and Wozniak 2011).

The factors of homophily, continuity over the lifetime, and continuity across generations also help to explain why some characteristics that have an important effect on many aspects of life do not make much difference for opinions. For example, research has found that unemployment does not have much effect on political opinions: most people continue to think and vote as they had before becoming unemployed (Schlozman and Verba 1979). This point can be explained by the weakness of homophily associated with unemployment. People who have a job work alongside other people with the same job and talk about matters of common concern; people who are unemployed have no occasion to communicate with each other. Moreover, most unemployed people regard their position as a temporary one and seek to make it as short as possible. As a result, they are likely to think of themselves in terms of their previous occupation: for example, as an accountant who is temporarily out of work rather than as an unemployed person.

Age has a large effect on many aspects of life, but it has no consistent relationship to opinions, even on issues that are closely connected to the interests of age groups such as spending on Social Security. This absence can be explained by contact across generations: most people have parents, grandparents, children, or grandchildren whom they care about. Moreover, age status is not permanent: all old people were young once, and all young people know that they will someday be old unless they die first. As a result, people of different ages do not form distinct communities that think of themselves as having opposing interests.

At any given time, there are often opinion differences between younger and older people – for example, support for same-sex marriage is higher among younger people. These differences, however, are mostly a matter of generation rather than age: that is, they are characteristics of people born at a particular time, and they persist as those people become older. The reason that generation is a more important influence than age is that generation, and the experiences associated with it, lasts throughout the lifetime. For example, if someone was born in the 1950s and affected by the civil rights movement and the Vietnam War, the memory of those events may have a lasting impact on their opinions.

Finally, gender has a profound impact on most aspects of life, but until the 1970s, there was little difference in the voting patterns or opinions of men and women. In recent years, a "gender gap" has emerged in many nations, in which women give more support to parties of the left and take more liberal positions on most issues. However, the gender difference is still not one of the larger group differences. For example, in the American presidential election of 2016, 41 percent of women and 54 percent of men reported voting for Donald Trump, a difference of thirteen percent. By comparison, eight percent of blacks and 58 percent of non-Hispanic whites voted for Trump, a difference of fifty percent. Moreover, there is little difference between the opinions of men and women on some issues that seem closely connected to gender. In 2016, the General Social Survey asked if a pregnant woman should be allowed to obtain a legal abortion "if she wants it for any reason": there was virtually no gender difference, with 44 percent of women and 45 percent of men agreeing that she should. There is a good deal of homophily associated with gender, and it remains the same over one's life. However, there is no continuity between generations: men can have daughters and women can have sons. Since families contain people of different sexes, most people communicate regularly with and care about members of the other gender. Like people of different ages, the different genders do not form distinct communities.

Some qualities have clear dividing lines: for example, in the United States the distinction between black and white is universally recognized. Although some individuals may be difficult to place, there is general agreement on the importance of the division. With religion, there is an institutional structure to provide boundaries: for example, Protestant or Catholic. Some other qualities, however, are more difficult to categorize. For example, it is agreed that there are important differences among different parts of the

United States, but there is no generally accepted way of classifying the regions. Moreover, place can be defined more or less broadly: a city contains many different neighborhoods, and a larger region contains different states and cities. All of these levels are potentially relevant for opinions: for example, in the United States, opinions are generally more conservative in the South compared to the North, in upstate New York compared to New York City, and in Staten Island compared to the other boroughs of New York City.

The measurement of social class raises special issues. Many different characteristics have been used to define class, including occupation, income, whether one is an employer or an employee, education, and others, and these characteristics have been combined in a variety of ways. Some observers treat class as essentially a matter of degree, in which positions are ranked from highest to lowest. Others regard class as a set of categories which do not necessarily have a clear ranking, raising the questions of how many classes there are and where their boundaries should be drawn. Some of these issues will be discussed later in this chapter, but for many purposes it is enough to make a rough distinction between the "working class," which includes manual and lower-level white-collar workers, and the "middle class," which includes executives, managers, and professionals.

The Direction of Group Differences

The factors of social interaction discussed in the previous section help to explain why group differences of opinion exist, but they do not explain the direction of those differences. For example, saying that opinions on the death penalty differ among ethnic groups does not tell us which groups are more in favor and which are more opposed. Some group differences can be explained by material interests: groups that are worse off can be expected to favor measures that promote equality and groups that are better off can be expected to oppose them. As Lipset (1960, p. 239) put it, "leftist parties represent themselves as instruments of social change in the direction of equality; the lower-income groups support them in order to become economically better off, while the higher-income groups oppose them in order to maintain their economic advantages."

Material interests are especially relevant to class differences, but also help to explain opinion differences among ethnic and religious groups. People who belong to groups that are worse off tend to favor measures that promote economic and social equality. That is, members of a group pay attention to the interests of other members of their group, as well as their individual interests. For example, the General Social Survey includes a question asking respondents to place themselves on a five-point scale running from "the government . . . should do everything possible to improve the standard of living of all poor Americans" to "each person should take care of himself." Support for the "government should do everything possible" position was 35 percent among blacks, 25 percent among Latinos, and only 12 percent among non-Hispanic whites. The ethnic differences exist even when comparing people with the same incomes.

Regional differences in material well-being, however, do not have a straightforward connection to opinions. In the contemporary United States, Republican support is higher in the poorer states, and this relationship seems to be growing stronger rather than weaker. Lipset (1960, p. 274) suggested that there was a general tendency for poor regions to be more conservative. He attributed this pattern to the persistence of traditional social relations, in which poor people paid little attention to politics and followed the lead of local elites. However, this explanation is not applicable to the contemporary United States, where even the poorest areas are exposed to the mass media and fully integrated into a market economy. Other observers hold that regional differences in opinion can endure for long periods of time, so that contemporary differences may be the result of historical factors from the distant past (Axelrod 1997). For example, Putnam (1993) holds that differences among Italian regions have endured since the Middle Ages, and Fischer (1991) argues that differences among American regions were established in the colonial period. Although there are many studies of regional differences of opinion in particular nations, there do not seem to have been any systematic comparative studies. Consequently, although it is clear that there are regional differences in opinion, it is not possible to generalize about the pattern of those differences.

Values – beliefs about right and wrong, or about how people should live their lives – are also an influence on opinions. Although values are complex and have many different aspects, it is possible to make a general distinction between "traditionalists" and "individualists." Traditionalists believe that there are absolute standards of right and wrong that apply to all people, while individualists believe that people should make their own choices. Individualism goes with support for policies such as equal rights for gays and lesbians, gender equality, and legalized abortion. Education, especially higher education, is associated with individualist values (Weakliem 2002; Svallfors 2005). Religion is also an important influence: people who are more religiously observant tend to be traditionalists, while those who are less observant tend to be individualists. Although there may be some differences among religions – for example, it is sometimes said that Protestants tend to be more individualistic than Catholics – the degree of observance seems to be the more important factor, at least in the contemporary world. Support for individualism is generally higher in cities than in rural areas. Cities tend to be more diverse, with a greater variety of cultures and lifestyles, and offer nonconformists more opportunity to find supportive communities (Wirth 1938). As a result, residents of cities are more tolerant of differences and may even see them as a positive good. Moreover, these features of urban life mean that new ideas are more likely to appear in cities, so that the opinion differences between urban and rural areas are continually renewed (Fischer 1978).

The boundaries between material interests and values are not exact. People generally see their values and interests as aligned: what is good for them is morally justified and good for society as a whole. This may be a matter of rationalizing their own interests: "men come easily to believe that arrangements agreeable to themselves are beneficial to others" (Dicey 1914, pp. 14–15). However, the connection may go in the other direction: people may persuade themselves that measures which they regard as right in principle or good for the community will benefit them. For example, a person with a high income who favored spending on programs to help the poor might say that her position was a matter of enlightened self-interest, on the grounds that reducing poverty would reduce crime and other social problems and increase economic growth. In general, it is not possible to say whether values or perceived interests come first: the important point is that they usually go together. Although it is hard to draw a precise line between values and interests, the distinction is still useful. For example, it seems safe to say that values, rather than material interests, are the primary influence on opinions about the death penalty. In contrast, material interests are likely to be an important influence on opinions about tax policy.

In addition to these general influences, group differences in opinion can be shaped by specific historical factors. Kaufman and Kaliner (2011) offer a case study of this process. In the past few decades, the neighboring states of Vermont and New Hampshire, although both predominantly rural and overwhelmingly white, have followed different courses in politics, with Vermont becoming one of the most strongly Democratic states, while New Hampshire remains evenly balanced between the parties and has a "libertarian" bent. Kaufman and Kaliner (2011) argue that this divergence does not reflect any single factor, but a combination of several causes. Once the states began to acquire different reputations, people with more liberal views chose to move to Vermont and those with more conservative views chose to move to New Hampshire, further accentuating the differences.

Axelrod (1997, p. 174) notes that the possibility of self-selection reinforces the tendency toward group homogeneity that results from social interaction. Self-selection is relevant not only to regional differences in opinion, but also to differences among occupations and religions, and between urban and rural areas. For example, a survey by the Pew Research Center found that liberals tended to prefer densely populated and walkable communities, while conservatives preferred less densely populated communities with larger houses (DeSilver 2014).

Persistence and Change in Group Differences

The processes of social interaction tend to maintain group differences even after the political and social conditions that produced them have changed. As children, people acquire a preference for a political party; later they adopt the opinions favored by that party and eventually pass their party preference on to their own children. The connection between party preference and opinions on specific issues is facilitated by the existence of "party images" (Milne and Mackenzie 1959, pp. 126–30). For example, the Democrats have an image of being concerned with the interests of the middle and working classes, and the Republicans have an image of being "tough" on foreign policy and committed to low taxes. These images, which can be learned at an early age, will make people more receptive to adopting the positions associated with the party. If party preferences were simply an inheritance from parents, group differences would gradually fade from generation to generation, but homophily means the views acquired from parents will also be reinforced by family and friends. As a result, group differences in opinion can persist long after the original causes have disappeared.

For example, in the United States, white Catholics and Jews give more support to the Democrats and have more liberal opinions on most issues than do white Protestants. These differences are hard to explain in terms of contemporary politics and society: in fact, Jews now have higher incomes than gentiles, on the average, so one might expect them to be more conservative on economic issues. However, they can be understood in terms of history: in the late nineteenth and early twentieth centuries, when the United States had a wave of immigration, mostly Jewish and Catholic, the Democrats were more sympathetic and favored policies to help the new immigrants. As a result, Catholics and Jews supported the Democrats, and this loyalty was passed on to successive generations.

Although social interaction usually promotes stability in group differences, it can sometimes facilitate rapid change. In any group, there are "opinion leaders" – people who are respected for being well informed and having good judgment (Berelson, Lazarsfeld, and McPhee 1954, p. 109). If opinion leaders change their minds, other members of the group will follow along. Moreover, social interaction can produce a "cascade" effect when an opinion that had been taken for granted is challenged (Kuran 1995). Some people who had previously had doubts but remained silent will realize that they are not alone and will speak up. As they hear opposing views, some people who had simply followed the prevailing opinion without questioning will begin to waver. Under these circumstances, the social pressure that had once supported the traditional opinion might quickly collapse, or switch toward favoring a different view.

An example of rapid change in group differences is the 1964 presidential election in the United States. Until that time, the Republicans had usually received about 25 percent of the black vote in presidential elections. However, in July 1964, a major civil rights act was passed with strong support from Lyndon Johnson, the Democratic President; shortly afterwards, the Republicans nominated a candidate who had vigorously opposed the act. In the election of November 1964, Republican support among black voters dropped to near zero, while many white Southerners who had traditionally voted for the Democrats switched to the Republicans. This rapid change in voting patterns was made possible by the visibility of the issue and its clear relationship to group interests. Even people who did not pay much attention to politics could get a sense of which party was "on their side" and could tell that something important was at stake in the election. The 1964 election produced a new equilibrium: since that time, the Republican share of the black vote has remained below ten percent and shown little change from one election to the next.

The Combination of Group Memberships

Any person can be regarded as the member of many different groups: for example, a white Catholic working-class woman who lives in a city. This fact raises a question of how the different

34

group memberships combine to influence opinions. One possibility is that the effects are additive: for example, if members of the working class tend to be on the left, and members of an ethnic minority group also tend to be on the left, then members of the working class who belong to the minority group will be farthest to the left, members of the middle class who belong to the the majority group will be farthest to the right, and members of the middle class who belong to the minority group and members of the working class who belong to the majority group will be somewhere in the middle. If effects are additive, group differences will be uniform: for example, class differences will be equally large among all ethnic groups, and ethnic differences will be equally large among all classes.

An alternative possibility is that group memberships combine in more complicated ways. In statistical language, this is an "interaction effect," where the size of a group difference depends on some other characteristic: for example, class differences might be larger in some ethnic groups than in others. Many researchers have found examples of interaction effects involving voting or opinions. For example, MacRae (1967, p. 257) found that, in the United States, social class had less effect on voting choices in rural areas than in cities. Weakliem and Biggert (1999) found that regional differences in a variety of opinions were smaller among blacks and Catholics. More recently, Gelman et al. (2009) found that the effect of income on voting choices was smaller in more affluent states; alternatively, one could say that regional differences were larger among people with higher incomes.

Despite the number of studies that consider interaction effects, there have been only a few attempts to offer a general explanation about when interaction effects occur and what form they will take. The most prominent one was offered by Lipset (1970, pp. 214–15), who proposed that people who are in an ambiguous position will tend to identify with the higher status group. For example, someone who has a working-class occupation and belongs to the dominant ethnic group will generally identify with the ethnic group; someone who has a middle-class occupation and is a member of the minority group will identify with the middle class. Thus, only people who are low on *both* statuses – members of the ethnic minority with working-class occupations – will tend to support the left. Another way to put this is that ethnic differences in party support will be larger in the working class than in the middle class, and class differences will be larger in the minority group than in the majority group.

Lipset (1970, p. 215) saw one major exception to his proposed rule: if the members of some group were rejected by the dominant high-status groups. Regardless of their other qualities, they would be treated the same as other members of their group, so they would continue to identify with that group. This is similar to Hughes's (1945) idea of a "master status" that overrides all other qualities. American blacks could be regarded as an example of this pattern: all classes give overwhelming support to the Democrats and take liberal positions on many issues.

Although the idea that people will identify with the higher status group seems plausible, there are many cases in which it does not hold. For example, one implication of this principle is that the opinions of people who experience upward social mobility will be similar to those in their current class, and the opinions of those who experience downward mobility will be similar to those in their class of origin. That is, both a person who grew up in a middle-class family and now has a working-class job and a person who grew up in a working-class family and now has a middle-class job will tend to follow the middle class rather than the working class. There has been a good deal of research on this question, and in general the opinions of people who have experienced either upward or downward mobility are about midway in between those of their origin and current class (Weakliem 2015). Overall, it is difficult to offer any generalization: research finds that the effects of different group memberships are sometimes additive and sometimes involve interaction. The question of when interaction effects do or do not appear is an important one that has not been adequately addressed.

The question of how different group memberships combine with each other can also apply at the societal level. The strength of regional, ethnic, religious, and class divisions clearly differs among societies – for example, class differences in party support have traditionally been smaller in the United States than in Britain. It has often been suggested that there is a connection among the strength of different divisions – for example, that the importance of ethnicity, region, and religion in American politics has reduced class differences (Alford 1963). Lijphart (1979) proposed that class differences are large only when religious and ethnic differences are absent – either because the society is homogeneous with respect to those characteristics, or because they have been taken out of politics. Similarly, Geertz (1963, p. 109) speaks of "primordial attachments," which include "contiguities of blood, speech, custom." He suggests that these primordial attachments can prevent people from developing attachments to more abstract identities such as class or nation. As these examples suggest, many observers have a sense that class differences are particularly sensitive to other factors. As with the individual level, however, there has not been a systematic attempt to examine the evidence – there are suggestive examples, but no comprehensive overview.

Industrialization and the Rise of Class

The general principle that opinions are formed as a result of social interaction implies that social changes which affect the patterns of interaction will also affect the nature and size of group differences in opinion. One of the first findings of survey research was that, in almost all nations, support for parties of the left was higher in the working class than in the middle class. Although class was certainly not the only factor that influenced party support, it had the most consistent and often the strongest effects. Lipset (1960, p. 230) said "in every modern democracy conflict among different groups is expressed through political parties which basically represent a 'democratic translation of the class struggle.'"

Although differences of economic conditions have existed in all societies, class does not seem to have been a major influence on political alignments until the twentieth century. For much of the nineteenth century, Britain and the United States had competitive elections based on a reasonably wide franchise, but none of the major parties regularly emphasized issues of economic equality, and class does not seem to have been a major influence on voting – region, religion, and ethnicity were the leading factors. It was not until the late nineteenth and early twentieth centuries that social class became an important source of political division.

As discussed in Chapter 1, public opinion surveys did not appear until the 1930s, so there is no precise information on how public opinion changed during the process of industrialization and urbanization in Western Europe and the United States. However, it is possible to offer an account that fits the general contours of the historical record (Weakliem and Adams 2011). Before the rise of industry, most poor people were farmers who worked by themselves or hired themselves out to landowners. They lived in villages or small towns, where they had contact with the local middle and upper classes, but not with poor people in other parts of the nation. Although an individual farmer could hope to improve his own condition by saving money and acquiring more land, there was little that small farmers could do collectively to advance their common interests. In the words of Karl Marx (1852[1969], p. 478) "the small-holding peasants form an enormous mass whose members live in similar conditions but without entering into manifold relations with each other. Their mode of production isolates them from one another instead of bringing them into mutual intercourse." Even the urban poor were mostly self-employed or provided personal services to people in the middle and upper classes. As a result, the lower classes were not a political force – if they were involved in politics at all, they followed the guidance of local elites rather than pursuing their class interests.

With the rise of industry, people who had previously been scattered were gathered together in cities and towns and worked side-by-side in factories. These changes meant they had more contact with other manual workers and less with members of the middle class. Moreover, their relationship to the middle class changed. The difference between a poor farmer and a prosperous landowner was just a matter of degree – the poor farmer might hope to gradually improve his situation by acquiring more land. In contrast, there was a qualitative difference between an employer and a factory worker – an employee could not gradually transform himself into a factory owner. As individuals, most workers had little control over their wages – they simply had to accept the going rate. However, they could advance their common interests by uniting against their employers, and this action was more effective if it was coordinated with action by workers in other parts of the country: as a result, workers sought to form labor unions. Efforts to unionize almost necessarily led to political involvement, because their chances of success were affected by laws governing unions and collective bargaining. The growth of labor unions was closely connected to the growth of socialist and labor parties in Europe. Although socialist parties never had much role in the United States, labor unions endorsed candidates and tried to influence legislation. During the 1930s the Democratic Party became more closely associated with policies of government aid to poor people and support for organized labor – in effect, it became more like a social democratic party. By the middle of the twentieth century, politics in almost all democratic nations revolved around the conflict between business and labor.

The implication of this account is that prevailing opinion in the lower classes changed during the course of industrialization. Rather than accepting inequality as inevitable, they came to regard it as an injustice and supported parties that promised to reduce it. One result of this process was an increase in class differences of opinion on economic issues, as the working class moved to the left. Another was a move to the left in average opinion, both because of the shift in working-class opinion and because some members of the middle classes were influenced by that shift, or at least became more willing to make concessions.

From Industrial to Post-Industrial Society

As economic development continued, there was a shift from manufacturing to services. The number of professionals and white-collar workers increased, while the number of factory workers declined. Average levels of formal education increased, and the number of people who worked for the government increased because of greater demand for education, health care, and other social services. The average size of organizations increased, so that there were more layers of managerial and supervisory workers rather than a sharp distinction between workers and capitalists (Dahrendorf 1959). Beginning in the 1970s, many observers spoke of a transition from "industrial" to "post-industrial" society (Touraine 1971; Bell 1973). This change should be thought of as a continuous process rather than a one-time shift: the process of "post-industrialization" is still going on. Many different ideas were offered about how the transition to post-industrial society would affect the pattern of group differences in politics, but they can be classified into four basic categories: a general decline of group differences, a decline of class differences, a shift in the nature of class differences, and no consistent change.

Decline of Group Differences

One view was that post-industrial society would bring a general decline of all group differences. The development of the mass media reduced the importance of face-to-face contact as a source of news and opinion, and meant that the great majority of people were exposed to the same ideas and information. Moreover, improvements in transportation meant that people could live farther from their place of work, so that different types of social relationships were less likely to overlap: neighbors were less likely to be workmates. Finally, people became more used to making individual choices, partly because a growth in education and the development of the mass media broadened their horizons, and partly because of experience in choosing among consumer goods. These changes meant that people would increasingly rely on their own judgment rather than following the lead of those around them: the individual would become more important relative to the group. This analysis was summarized in the title of a book by Rose and McAllister (1986): *Voters Begin to Choose.*

Decline of Class Differences

A second view was that the development of post-industrial society would lead to a decline of class divisions, but not of other group divisions. One reason that class differences might decline was a change in working conditions. In manufacturing industries, workers tended to form an "isolated mass" (Kerr and Siegel 1954). They worked in large groups under similar conditions, subject to common discipline from the employer, and had little contact with other classes. Under these circumstances, workers "not only have the same grievances, but they have them at the same time, at the same places, and against the same people" (Kerr and Siegel 1954, p. 192). Service workers, in contrast, interact with customers or clients, who are often from the middle or upper classes. Their pay and experience of work are affected by their relations with customers. Moreover, service workers often work part-time or have irregular hours, so that they do not have regular contact with their fellow employees. As a result, service workers are less likely to develop class consciousness and are more open to influence from the middle class. Even within manufacturing, there has been a shift to more differentiation of jobs and more flexible work arrangements, so that fewer workers are part of a large group performing simple repetitive tasks. As a result of these changes, workers may focus on individual rather than collective advancement.

A second potential reason for the decline of class differences was general affluence. Some observers argued that as standards of living increased, material needs would be less pressing, and people would give higher priority to other concerns such as values or social status. In effect, this analysis holds that non-material concerns are luxury goods: people give higher priority to them after their material needs are satisfied (Inglehart 1997). This analysis suggested that class differences would decline, but that other group differences might increase. Religious differences – particularly the differences between more and less religious people – could be expected to become more prominent, since religion is related to values. Ethnic divisions might increase as previously marginalized groups demanded greater status and respect (Bell 1975). For similar reasons, divisions involving gender and sexual identity could become increasingly important.

A third possible reason was the growth of the state. Hechter (2004) argued that government social programs weakened the labor movement because the government supplied services that unions had traditionally provided, such as health insurance and unemployment benefits. At the same time, the government became increasingly involved in issues that had previously been left to families, private organizations, and local communities: for example, prohibiting discrimination by gender, ethnicity, or sexual orientation. As a result, the central political conflict shifted from class to "culture" (Hechter 2004).

Rise of New Class Divisions

A third view was that class divisions would change rather than simply decline. Traditionally, the distinction between manual and non-manual workers was important. Even manual workers who earned high wages because of special skills or strong union organization thought of themselves as "labor," while low-paid white-collar workers identified with "management." Stinchcombe (1989, p. 170) proposed that the growth of government welfare programs meant that income differences would become more important, while the difference between manual and non-manual status became less important: "class conflict in modern societies is no longer about capitalism but about income distribution." The primary reason for this development was the growth of government welfare programs: taxes and benefits are primarily based on income rather than on occupation. For example, skilled blue-collar workers who faced high taxes might increasingly think of themselves as "taxpayers" rather than as workers.

Grusky and Sorensen (1998) argued that differences among broad categories such as manual or non-manual would decline, but that differences among narrowly defined occupational groups would grow. One reason for this development was that licensing requirements and other kinds of government regulation could affect the interests of specific occupational groups. A second was the rise in levels of education and training, much of which is specific to particular occupations. For example, lawyers, doctors, and research scientists might develop different outlooks as a result of their different training and work experience. Moreover, as specific occupations develop different reputations, people will tend to go into those that suit their values and interests. Consequently, the differences among different occupations with roughly the same skill or income levels will increase.

No Change

A final possibility was that the shift to post-industrial society would have little or no effect on class differences in opinion. Despite the economic and social changes, some people are still better off than others in terms of income, working conditions, and job security. In fact, overall income differences have tended to increase since the 1970s. Consequently, the material basis for class differences of opinion about whether social inequality should be reduced is still present. If anything, the differences might become stronger as the status distinction between manual and non-manual workers fades. In the past, white-collar workers often thought of themselves as an elite group, and identified with management rather than manual workers. As white-collar workers became more numerous and fewer had serious prospects of moving into the higher levels of management, this sense of distinctiveness would decline, and lower level white-collar workers would come to think of themselves as part of the working class (Goldthorpe 1987).

Changes in Voting Patterns

Class

There have been many studies of "class voting" – that is, class differences in party support. Until the mid-1960s, the consensus was that these differences were either holding steady or gradually increasing, but in the 1970s a number of studies reported a decline (Lipset 1981). The claim of a decline in class voting was debated over the next few decades. Some observers argued that there was a general decline, while others held that there was short-term variation without any definite trend (see Clark and Lipset 2001, and Evans 1999, for overviews of the debate).

Subsequent experience has made it clear that there have been some general trends in the political tendencies of different occupational groups. Professionals have shifted to the left, to the point that support for parties of the left is sometimes higher among professionals than among manual workers. There have been smaller shifts to the left among managers and lower-level white-collar workers. Manual workers have shifted toward the right, and supply many of the votes for "new right" parties such as the National Rally in France. Self-employed people and small proprietors have traditionally been on the right, and have remained there.

Jansen, Evans, and De Graaf (2013, p. 71), after reviewing changes in fifteen nations, conclude that "social class has undeniably weakened as a basis of left–right party choice." The changes that they discuss could be described as a transformation of class voting rather than a decline: there are still occupational differences in party choice. However, the differences that have grown are "horizontal" ones involving groups with similar levels of income and social standing – for example, between managers and professionals – while those that have declined are "vertical" ones – for example, between professionals and manual workers. Thus, the generalization that "lower" occupational standing goes with higher support for parties of the left is less accurate than it was in the middle of the twentieth century.

It is also clear that there have been changes in the effects of university education. In the middle of the twentieth century, higher education was associated with greater support for conservative parties, even after taking account of income and occupation. That is, if one compared two people with the same income and occupation, the one with university education was more likely to support conservative parties. However, this effect became smaller and then changed direction: today, when comparing people with the same income and occupation, those who have university degrees are more likely to support parties of the left (van der Waal, Achterberg, and Houtman 2007; Piketty 2018). The changes in the effect of higher education help to account for the changes among occupational groups: the groups that have moved to the left are the most highly educated ones.

Several studies have examined changes in the relationship between income and party choice. Bartels (2008, pp. 73–8) argued that the relationship between income and party choice in the United States increased between the 1950s and the early twenty-first century. Weakliem (2013) came to similar conclusions, although his analysis suggested that the influence of income leveled off after the 1980s rather than continuing to increase. Piketty (2018) found that income differences in party support had stayed about the same in Britain, declined slightly in the United States, and declined more substantially in France. In a study of fifteen nations, van der Waal, Achterberg, and Houtman (2007) found that income differences in party support had increased in most of them. Despite the differences, in a larger sense these studies all lead to the same conclusion: that changes involving income have been smaller and less consistent than those involving occupation and education.

There are no systematic studies of the hypothesis of increasing divergence among specific occupations. Most surveys classify occupation into a small number of broad occupational categories, which sometimes change over time or differ among surveys conducted by different organizations. As a result, studies that combine data from different surveys must reduce them to a least common denominator containing only a few categories. The General Social Survey, and similar surveys in other nations, distinguish among a large number of occupational categories, but the numbers in most of the occupations are small, making estimates subject to a high degree of sampling error. However, the prospects for evaluating this hypothesis are improving as more data accumulate.

Other Factors

Religious differences in party choice seem to have followed different courses in different nations. In the United States, the difference between Catholics and Protestants has declined, but the difference between more and less religious people has increased. That is, the Republicans now do better among more religious people of all faiths. In a sense, the United States is moving toward a pattern that has existed in some European countries for many years, in which the main conflict is between clericalism and anti-clericalism. In contrast, Piketty (2018) finds a decline in voting differences between practicing Catholics and non-believers in France since the 1960s. The growth of the Muslim population has created a new religious division in many European nations. Muslims generally favor the left parties, and this tendency may be growing stronger: in the French presidential election of 2012, about 90 percent of Muslims voted for the left (Piketty 2018).

In the United States, voting differences between blacks and whites increased in the election of 1964, and have remained roughly constant since that time. Asian-Americans and Hispanics also give large majorities to the Democrats, and there is no sign that they are declining. In Europe, ethnic differences are closely linked to religion, since most immigrants from Africa, the Middle East, and Asia are Muslim. Immigrants from non-European backgrounds generally support parties of the left, and the growth in their numbers means that these differences are becoming more important for political life.

Changes in regional differences have received less systematic attention than changes in class, ethnic, or religious differences, but there appears to be no general decline. In some cases, including the United States, they have increased.

Finally, gender differences have grown in many nations. In the 1950s, there was little difference between the voting patterns of men and women in some nations, such as the United States; in other nations, such as France and Italy, women gave more support to conservative parties. Since the 1960s, women have generally moved toward the left, either reversing the traditional pattern or creating a new "gender gap." This shift seems to be partly the result of economic changes: increased female participation in labor force, later marriage, and greater frequency of divorce means that women have more reason to support social programs and government action to increase their opportunities at work (Manza and Brooks 1999). It may also reflect general cultural changes: the rise of feminism after the 1960s has made women less willing to accept inequalities that were once regarded as natural or inevitable.

Interpreting the Changes

Although there are differences among specific nations, some general points are clear. Political differences between a broadly defined "working class" and "middle class" have declined. Some parts of the middle class, particularly professionals, have moved to the left, while at least some manual workers have moved to the right. This change is partly due to a shift in the effect of higher education. Since these trends have occurred in many nations and continued over a long period of time, they are likely to reflect general social and economic changes, rather than factors specific to particular nations or elections. Second, there has not been a general decline of group differences in voting. Some differences have declined, but others have remained the same, while others have increased.

Many observers have suggested that the changes involving occupation and education can be explained by changes in the relative importance of economic and "social" issues. Research from the 1940s and 1950s found that more-educated people were more tolerant of ethnic minorities, more internationalist in foreign affairs, and more likely to support civil liberties for people with unpopular views (Stouffer 1955). On economic issues, however, education was associated with more conservative views (Key 1961). These facts suggest that when social issues became more important in politics, educated people will shift to the left. During the 1960s and 1970s, questions such as gender equality and the treatment of gays and lesbians became the subject of controversy. In the United States, issues related to racial equality received more attention, and the positions of the parties on these issues became more clearly distinguished. Since that time, growing ethnic diversity has made questions of multiculturalism and ethnic relations more prominent in many nations. Finally, Kitschelt and Rehm (2019) observe that as the number of people with college education increased, political parties had more incentive to advocate the positions that were popular among them.

The Relative Importance of Social and Economic Opinions

The hypothesis of a change in the relative importance of economic and social issues can be evaluated by examining the association between opinions and voting choices in different elections. Figure 2.1 shows the correlations of opinions on four issues with Democratic versus Republican voting (third-party candidates are omitted) in American presidential elections from 1972 to 2016. The questions are whether the government should try to reduce income differences between the rich and the poor, whether it is the responsibility of the government to help people pay for doctors and hospital bills, whether the government has a special obligation to help improve the living standards of African-Americans, and whether a pregnant woman should be able to obtain an abortion if she wants one for any reason. The first two would usually be classified as economic issues, and the third and fourth as social issues. A positive correlation means that people with liberal opinions, as conventionally defined, are more likely to vote for the Democratic candidate. The size of the correlation indicates the strength of the association – a correlation of 1.0 would mean that all people with liberal opinions voted for the Democrat and all people with conservative opinions voted for the Republican.

The correlations of all four opinions with vote have increased over time, but the increase is particularly large for abortion. In

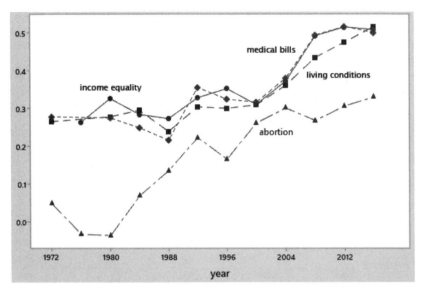

Figure 2.1 Correlation of Opinions with Democratic/Republican Voting, 1972–2016

Source: compiled with data from the General Social Survey

the 1970s, the correlations involving abortion were near zero – supporters and opponents of abortion were about equally likely to support the Republican candidate. By the end of the period, the correlations involving abortion were almost as large as those involving the other issues.

The four questions considered in Figure 2.1 are only a small selection of the possible issues, but the results give support to the hypothesis that the importance of social issues has increased. Moreover, the analysis does not begin until 1972, and there is evidence that the importance of opinions about race grew during the 1960s (Carmines and Stimson 1989). At the same time, the importance of traditional economic issues for voting choices has not declined, contrary to Inglehart's (1997) idea of a shift from material to non-material concerns.

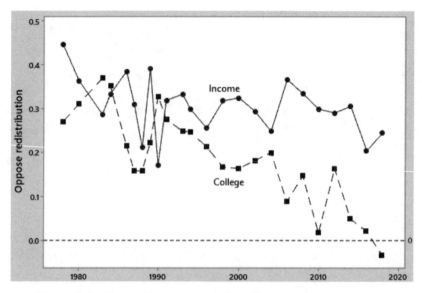

Figure 2.2 Effects of Income and College Degree on Opinions about Redistribution

Source: compiled with data from the General Social Survey

Education and Economic Opinions

Most attempts to explain changes in class voting focus on changes in the relative importance of economic and social issues, and do not consider the possibility of changes in class differences of opinion on those issues. For example, Kitschelt and Rehm (2019) say that "we will assume that the political preferences of . . . education-income groups are relatively stable over time." However, there is some evidence of changes in the effect of education on opinions. Figure 2.2 shows estimates of the effects of college education and family income on answers to the GSS question about whether the government should try to reduce income differences. Positive values mean that higher values of education or income go with more conservative opinions. When the question was first asked in 1978, higher levels of both income and education were associated with more conservative opinions. As time went on, the effect of income declined only slightly, but the effect of higher education declined rapidly. In 2016, it was actually negative – that is, a person with a college degree was slightly more favorable to redistribution than a person who had the same income but lacked a college degree. A similar pattern is found for opinions about government aid to the poor. That is, educated people have moved in a liberal direction on at least some economic issues, and changes in class voting are not entirely a result of changes in the relative importance of different kinds of issues.

Summary and Conclusions

The model proposed by Berelson, Lazarsfeld, and McPhee (1954) still offers a useful framework for understanding public opinion. Its basic principle is that our opinions are not entirely our own – to a large extent, they are borrowed from the people around us. The model helps to explain why there are group differences in opinion that can endure for a long period of time but sometimes change rapidly, and why particular groups have a larger or smaller impact on opinions.

The model suggests that general social changes will affect the pattern of group differences. The chapter discussed hypotheses about the ways that industrialization and the subsequent development of "post-industrial society" may have affected group differences, especially those involving social class. It is difficult adequately to test all of these hypotheses, since they involve changes over a long period of time, but there is clear evidence for one development: educated people are more likely to support parties of the left than they were in the past. Thus, the relationship between party and class has become more complex: it is no longer accurate simply to say that the "lower classes" support the left and the "upper classes" support the right.

Understanding the changing relationship between education and party support is an important issue for research. One popular idea is that it reflects a rise in the relative importance of "social" issues, on which education is associated with more liberal opinions. There is some evidence of a rise in the importance of social issues, but there is also evidence of a change in the relationship between education and economic opinions: specifically, highly educated people have become more sympathetic to redistribution. The reasons for this change are not well understood:

3

Ideology

Political views are often described in terms of an ideological spectrum. One end is known as the left, progressive, or (in the United States) liberal; the other as the right or conservative. A popular definition of left and right, which is implicit in the terms "progressive" and "conservative," is that the left favors change while the right favors the status quo, or a return to the past. Of course, conservatives sometimes call for a change from current policies, but when they do they usually present it as a restoration of some previous state of affairs. Another definition involves values: the reduction of inequality is a primary goal for the left, but not for the right (Lukes 2003). Although the right does not regard inequality as a good thing in itself, it sees it as the necessary price of some other desirable goals such as freedom or economic growth, or as the result of individual choices.

In most democratic countries, it is possible to classify the leading parties on this spectrum, running from extreme left through moderate left, center, moderate right, and extreme right. On close examination, some parties are hard to place exactly, but it would be very difficult to discuss political parties without referring to left and right. Whether ideology is important to the general public, however, is a more difficult question. This chapter will discuss the degree to which the public thinks in terms of ideology, according to several different measures. It will then consider "polarization": the magnitude of ideological differences. Finally, it will examine differences between the nature of ideology in the parties and the public.

Recognition and Understanding of Ideological Terms

In most nations, large majorities are willing to locate their views on a left–right spectrum (Mair 2007). For example, the General Social Survey asks people to place themselves on a seven-point scale running from "extremely liberal" to "extremely conservative"; in 2016, about 27 percent chose one of the three liberal categories, 36 percent chose moderate, 34 percent chose one of the three conservative categories, and only four percent refused to answer or said that they could not choose. However, it is not clear how much these labels mean to people. Some surveys explicitly offer a chance to decline to answer, for example by adding "or haven't you given this much thought," and in this case usually about 20 to 25 percent of people choose that option.

Other surveys have asked people to characterize political parties in terms of left and right: for example, a 2005 survey asked whether one of the parties was more conservative than the other, and if so, which party was more conservative. Only 48 percent gave what would normally be regarded as the correct answer, that the Republicans were more conservative: 17 percent said the Democrats were more conservative, 17 percent said there was no difference, and 16 percent said that they did not know if one party was more conservative than the other. Some of the people who gave other answers may have been aware of the conventional view but disagreed with it. However, these answers were more common among less-educated people, suggesting that most of the people who gave them simply did not understand the ideological terms, at least not in the way that they are used by most political observers.

A few surveys have asked people to say what the terms "liberal" and "conservative" mean to them. With an open-ended question, there is room for judgment about how to classify the answers, so that it is not possible to offer precise estimates, but it is clear that only a minority define the terms with reference to policies or to political philosophies. Many people simply say that they do not know, while others refer to personal qualities – for example, that liberals are "open-minded" or conservatives are "thrifty." For example, in 2005 a survey asked "what do you think is the biggest difference between liberal views and conservative views?": four percent gave answers classified as "general attitude toward social change," four percent gave "general attitude towards government," and seven percent gave "general attitude toward money and economics." The largest single group, at 38 percent, was "don't know," while 32 percent gave answers that were classified as "personal characteristics and traits."

This evidence suggests that ideology is not very important to the American public. Most people recognize ideological terms and are willing to apply one to themselves, but in many cases that is just another way of declaring party preference: someone is a Republican, knows that the Republicans are supposed to be the more conservative party, and concludes that he must be conservative. Some people simply match their party with their preferred ideological term: someone who is a Democrat and thinks of herself as a conservative may conclude that the Democrats are the more conservative party.

In most European nations, the parties have traditionally had clearer ideological positions than in the United States, and some party names include ideological terms such as "conservative," "left," or "socialist." However, studies in France (Converse 1975, pp. 109–10) and Britain (Butler and Stokes 1974) came to the same conclusions as the American studies: most people seemed to have only a superficial understanding of ideology.

Symbolic and Operational Ideology

Nevertheless, it is possible that ideological identification can influence voting even if people do not understand the terms. Free and Cantril (1967) distinguished between "symbolic" and "operational" ideology. Operational ideology involves opinions on specific issues, while symbolic ideology involves general statements of principle about government and society. Identification of oneself as liberal or conservative is influenced by both symbolic and operational ideology. Free and Cantril argued that, in the United States, operational ideology was generally liberal but symbolic ideology was generally conservative: many people took liberal positions on most political issues but agreed with statements such as "the government has gone too far in regulating business and interfering with the free enterprise system." This pattern meant that the Republican Party had an advantage: some people who agreed with the Democrats on most issues would nevertheless be attracted by the rhetoric of the Republicans.

Whether "operational ideology" is actually liberal is open to debate. On the one hand, majorities favor increased spending on most domestic social programs. For example, the General Social Survey includes a number of questions about whether we are spending too much, too little, or about the right amount of money on various national problems. On twelve of the fifteen items involving domestic problems, a majority says that we are spending too little, and on two of the others, the support for the position we are spending too little is greater than support for the position that we are spending too much. There is also generally majority support for increasing the minimum wage and requiring employers to provide benefits such as health care or parental leave. Substantial majorities say that people with high incomes pay too little in taxes and that people with low and moderate incomes pay too much. On the other hand, there is generally strong support for tax cuts, even when most of the benefits go to people with high incomes (Bartels 2005; Graetz and Shapiro 2006). Moreover public opinion is clearly conservative on some "social issues," particularly those involving crime. In response to questions in the General Social Survey, over 75 percent say that the courts in their area are not harsh enough in dealing with criminals, and about 70 percent favor the death penalty for convicted murderers. Majorities generally support laws requiring long sentences for repeat offenders: for example, California's "three strikes" law, which requires life sentences with almost no chance or parole for a third felony conviction, was passed in a referendum with support from 70 percent of the voters. Support for civil liberties, including free speech, is often weak: in 2014, only 42 percent said "a Muslim clergyman who preaches hatred of the United States" should be allowed "to make a speech in your community." There are also issues on which public opinion seems to fall in the middle of the political spectrum: for example, majorities say that abortion should be legal in a fairly wide range of circumstances, but also support restrictions such as requiring parental approval for minors or banning some late-term abortions. Overall, it is difficult to characterize public opinion in general as liberal or conservative: it is liberal on some issues and conservative on others.

In terms of trends, however, there is a clear pattern: over the last fifty years or so, operational ideology has become more liberal by any reasonable definition. There are many issues on which average opinion has become more liberal, and very few on which it has become more conservative (see Chapter 4 for further discussion). At the same time, the number of people who call themselves conservatives has increased. Until the late 1960s, the number of self-described liberals and conservatives was about equal, but since that time, conservatives have consistently out-numbered liberals. Ellis and Stimson (2012) explain the shift toward conservative identification by noting that the "liberal" and "conservative" can be understood in terms of lifestyles and personal values. "Conservative" is associated with tradition and conventional standards, so if the terms are understood in this way, most people regard themselves as conservative. They suggest that cultural changes since the 1960s have focused attention on these non-political meanings, and therefore caused an increase in the number of people who called themselves conservative. Another possibility is that the growth of the state has made people more likely to support the general proposition that the government is too large and powerful, despite their approval of specific pro-grams. Some evidence of this is provided by a survey question that has been asked since the 1960s: "which of the following will be the biggest threat to the country in the future – big business, big labor, or big government?" The percentage who answer "big government" has increased since the 1970s, while the percentage who answer "big business" has stayed about the same (Fishman and Davis 2017).

Ideological self-identification is associated with voting choices: people with the same positions on specific issues are more likely to vote Republican if they call themselves conservative than if they call themselves liberal or moderate. Although some people may call themselves conservative because they vote Republican, it seems reasonable to think that at least some of the association is because people judge parties by their labels. The changing popularity of the terms definitely seems to have influenced the language used by the parties: since the 1970s, Republicans have often called Democrats "liberal," while Democrats have tried to avoid the term. Some Democratic candidates have downplayed ideological labels and focused on specific policies, while others have adopted alternative labels, especially "progressive."

Outside of the United States, the term "left" is more widely used, and "liberal" generally applies to parties of the center or sometimes the right (the major Australian conservative party is called the Liberal Party). The terms "left" and "right" do not have the associations with lifestyle and values that liberal and conservative do, and "left" seems to have more positive connotations – Mair (2007) points out that many parties have included "left" as part of their name, but few have included "right." Therefore, the historical analysis proposed by Ellis and Stimson (2012) applies only to the United States, but it raises a general point that applies more widely: "party images" can change as parties come to be associated with different groups or different values, and these changes can affect support for the parties, even apart from changes in opinions on specific issues.

Attitude Constraint

To this point, the discussion has considered the use and understanding of ideological labels. Another way to define ideology involves the associations among different opinions. Some issues are closely related by nature – for example, people who think that the government has a responsibility to help the poor could be expected to support more spending on social programs, since that is an obvious way to achieve their goal. But often views on one issue can be predicted from views on another issue that has no obvious connection – for example, in the contemporary United States, people who think that abortion should be legal tend to support more spending on environmental protection. Converse (1964) called the association among opinions "attitude constraint" and this term has been widely adopted by social scientists. One possible source of attitude constraint is party loyalty – people will tend to adopt the views advocated by the leaders of their party. A second is the existence of values or principles that influence opinions on a variety of issues. For example, a person who is inclined to respect authority might be more inclined to favor "traditional" gender roles and also to support management against labor unions.

Attitude constraint generally increases with education: in the General Social Survey, the correlation between opinions on whether abortion should be legal and spending on environmental protection is 0.05 among people who did not attend college and 0.12 among people with college degrees. It also increases with political interest and involvement – it is very strong among political elites, moderately strong among people who are active in politics, and weak among people who are not active (Converse 1975). For example, a Pew survey from 2014 contained questions on gun control ("what do you think is more important – to protect the right of Americans to own guns, or to control gun ownership?") and abortion ("do you think abortion should be legal in all or most cases, or illegal in all or most cases?"): the correlation between opinions on the two issues was 0.4 among people who said that they always voted, and 0.12 among people who said they sometimes or never did.

Polarization

Definitions of Polarization

Political polarization has recently received a great deal of attention in the United States. The prevailing view is that it has increased, although some observers hold that there has been little change (see Gentzkow 2016 for a review). Before considering the evidence on polarization, it is necessary to distinguish several meanings of the word. The first involves the distribution of opinions on individual questions: polarization means that many people have "extreme" rather than moderate views on a given issue. A second meaning is the strength of association between opinions and party identification. If both parties contain people with a variety of opinions on an issue, the difference of average opinions between the parties will be small. If opinion becomes more closely linked to party, the average difference of opinion between supporters of the two parties will increase, differences of opinion within each party will decline, and there will be less ideological overlap between the parties. A third meaning is the general degree of attitude constraint: that is, the strength of association between opinions on different opinions. If attitude constraint is low, any two people are likely to agree on some issues and disagree on others; if it is high, they are likely to agree or disagree across the board. Another way to put it is that, when attitude constraint is high, there will be more "consistent" liberals and conservatives, and fewer people who take liberal positions on some issues and conservative positions on others. A fourth meaning is negative feelings, such as dislike or distrust, between supporters of the different parties. There is no necessary relationship among any of these types of polarization, but it seems likely that there will be some connections among them. For example, a strong association between opinions and party means that members of different parties will have fewer occasions on which they work together, which could result in more negative feelings.

Consequences of Polarization

The different kinds of polarization do not necessarily have the same consequences. Strong feelings of animosity toward the other party and its supporters are clearly undesirable, but attitude constraint and the alignment of ideology and party could both be regarded as either positive or negative.

If candidates offer disconnected sets of positions on a large number of issues, it will be difficult for voters to make choices and difficult for politicians to interpret the outcome of elections. An ideology provides at least a rough guide for both voters and political leaders: voters can decide if they want to move left, right, or stay about the same, and the results of an election show what direction the majority preferred. On the other hand, strong attitude constraint among political elites means that the large number of voters who are liberal on some issues and conservative on others will not have their opinions well represented, and that elections may lead to consequences that voters do not want. For example, voters may support a conservative party because they think that taxes are too high, but get additional restrictions on abortion as well as lower taxes.

It is also possible that the effects of attitude constraint depend on its source. If it results from following convention or allegiance to a group, it may promote negative feelings and make compromise more difficult. As Bell (1962, p. 405) puts it, "ideology makes it unnecessary for people to consider individual issues on their individual merits. One simply turns to the ideological vending machine, and out comes the prepared formulae." However, attitude constraint can also be a result of the application of general principles, which might be a source of new ideas and approaches.

A weak alignment between ideology and party might limit feelings of animosity by creating ties between supporters of different parties – that is, two people who are members of different parties will agree on some issues and have reason to work together on them. However, it also means that voters may not have much sense of what they are voting for, unless they have detailed knowledge of the individual candidates. Moreover, ideological overlap may mean that policies depend on personal relations among politicians rather than the outcome of the election. Traditionally, there was little polarization between American political parties, and many obserers thought that it would be desirable to have more. In fact, the American Political Science Association issued a report calling for the parties to become more ideologically distinct (American Political Science Association 1950). It is possible that there is an ideal level of polarization – that both excessively low levels and excessively high levels are harmful – but it is difficult to measure or specify this level.

Changes in Polarization

It is difficult to judge trends in the presence of "extreme" opinions on individual issues. Most survey questions do not offer a choice between more and less extreme positions, but simply ask people to choose between two options. Some questions ask respondents to indicate the strength of agreement or disagreement, but strongly held opinions are not necessarily extreme opinions. For example, a person might be strongly in favor of an increase in the minimum wage, but believe that the increase should be a small one. In order to measure change in the distribution of moderate and extreme opinions, it is necessary to have questions that offer a choice among a range of possibilities and are repeated over a period of time. Such questions are relatively rare, but there are a few studies that have considered trends and found no general evidence of change (Dimaggio, Evans, and Bryson 1996; Fiorina and Abrams 2008). For example, the General Social Survey includes questions asking whether government spending on a number of areas should be increased, reduced, or kept about the same, and there is no clear trend in the number taking the "extreme" positions – increased or reduced rather than kept as is.

However, there is evidence of growing support for extreme positions on one important issue, abortion (Weakliem 2016). Figure 3.1 shows changes in opinions about whether abortion should be legal in different circumstances. Since the 1970s, support for the position that abortion should be allowed if "the woman wants it for any reason" has grown, but support for the position that abortion should be allowed if the pregnancy was a result of rape has declined. That is, support has grown for both extreme positions – that abortion should be allowed without restrictions and that it should never, or almost never, be allowed.

Opinion differences between supporters of different parties have certainly increased. Traditionally, American political parties

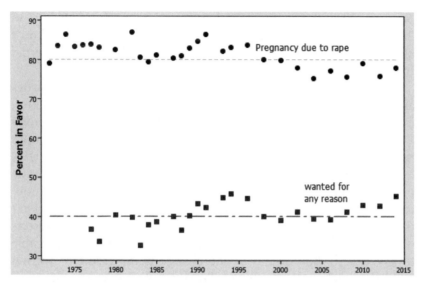

Figure 3.1 Percent in Favor of Legal Abortion under Different Circumstances

Source: compiled with data from the General Social Survey

Previously published in *The Washington Post*, February 19, 2016

were loose coalitions with a good deal of ideological overlap – both parties included significant numbers of people with liberal, moderate, and conservative opinions. However, since the 1960s, many conservative Democrats became Republicans while liberal and moderate Republicans became Democrats, so the ideological differences between parties have become larger. Among political elites, there is now almost complete ideological separation. The Americans for Democratic Action, a liberal organization, calculates scores ranging from zero to 100 for each member of Congress based on their votes on a number of key issues, with higher numbers indicating a more liberal voting record. In 1977, the average score was 57 for Democratic senators and 30 for Republican senators. Seven of the forty Republicans had scores over 60, and fifteen of the sixty Democrats had scores under 40. In 2016, the mean scores were 90 for Democrats and 7 for Republicans. No Republican had a score over 60, and only one Democrat had a score under 40. In 1977, 22 senators had scores between 40 and 60; in 2016 there were only three. That is, in 2016 almost all Democratic senators were reliable liberals, almost all Republicans were reliable conservatives, and very few senators from either party were moderates.

Ideological differences between supporters of the two parties are much smaller in the general public than among political elites, but they have clearly increased as well (Baldassarri and Gelman 2008). One reason for the increase is "sorting," as people choose the party that best fits their ideology. Another is that supporters of a party are influenced by party elites – that is, as Democratic politicians became more liberal and Republicans became more conservative, people have "followed the leader" (Lenz 2013). That is, supporters of the Democrats moved to the left and supporters of the Republicans moved to the right. Although it is not possible to say exactly how much of the change is the result of sorting and how much is the result of following political leaders, it seems likely that both are significant factors in the increased separation between parties.

The partisan divide has grown, not only on political issues, but also on some questions of personal values and morality. For example, the General Social Survey contains a question on whether it is wrong for a married person to have sex with someone other than their spouse. Republicans are more likely than Democrats to say that it is "always wrong," and the gap is now about twice as large as it was in the 1970s and 1980s. Like the shifts in liberal and conservative identification discussed by Ellis and Stimson (2012), this point suggests that there has been a change in the general images of the two parties.

Attitude constraint also has increased in recent decades, resulting in an increase in the number of "consistent" liberals and conservatives. For example, the correlation between opinions on legal abortion and on spending on environmental protection rose from 0.05 in the 1970s to 0.16 in 2010–2016. Boxell, Gentzkow, and Shapiro (2017) find that the average correlation among seven questions covering a range of political issues has grown steadily since the mid-1980s. A study by the Pew Research Center (2014) using a different set of questions, found that the number of "consistent" liberals and conservatives stayed about the same between 1994 to 2004, but doubled between 2004 and 2014. Thus, it is clear that there has been an increase in attitude constraint, but there is some question about the exact timing of the change.

Finally, although there are only a few survey questions measuring feelings of animosity to the other party and its supporters, or what Abramowitz and Webster (2016) call "negative partisanship," they all indicate that it has increased dramatically. In 1960, a survey asked people how they would feel if a son or daughter married a supporter of the other party. Only two percent said they would be "displeased"; seven percent said they would be pleased and ninety percent said that it would make no difference to them (Almond and Verba 1963). A 2008 survey asked a similar question offering "not at all upset," "somewhat upset," and "very upset" as possible responses: 20 percent of Democrats and 27 percent of Republicans said that they would be somewhat or very upset (Iyengar, Sood, and Lelkes 2012). This questions was repeated in 2017, and 14 percent said they would be somewhat or very upset if a son or daughter married someone from the opposite party. The same survey asked people how they would feel if a son or daughter married a supporter of Donald Trump (for Democrats) or an opponent (for Republicans): 33 percent said they would be somewhat or very upset. Despite the difference in question wording between 1960 and the recent surveys, it seems safe to say that negative reactions to the prospect of a child marrying a supporter of the other party have become much more common.

The 1960 and 2008 surveys also asked whether supporters of different parties were "intelligent" and "selfish." In 1960, 33 percent said that supporters of their own party were intelligent, and 27 percent said supporters of the other party were. In 2008, 62 percent said that supporters of their party were intelligent and only 14 percent said that supporters of the other party were. There was also a large increase in the number seeing supporters of the other party as selfish: from 21 percent in 1960 to 47 percent in 2008 (Iyengar, Sood, and Lelkes 2012).

Further evidence of a rise in negative partisanship comes from a question included in the American National Election Studies since

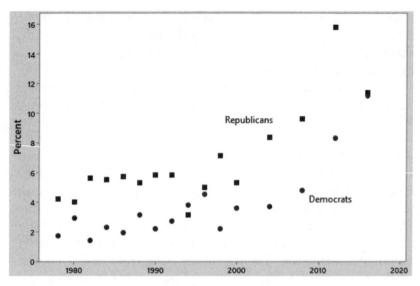

Figure 3.2 Percent Rating Democratic and Republican Parties at Zero

Source: compiled with data from American National Election Studies

1978: a "feeling thermometer" that asks people to rate whether they feel "favorable and warm" to each party on a scale of zero to 100. The gap between ratings of one's preferred party and the other party has grown over that period, mostly because of a rise in negative feelings about the other party. A particularly striking development is the increase in the number of extremely low ratings. Figure 3.2 shows the percent rating each party at zero. It increased gradually between 1978 and 2000, and more rapidly after 2000. In 1968, two percent rated the Democrats at zero and four percent rated the Republicans at zero; in 2016 the figures were 11 percent for both parties. In contrast, the percent rating the parties at 100 has fluctuated with no clear trend, averaging 5 about percent for the Republicans and ten percent for the Democrats. Until 2012, the combined number of 100 ratings always exceeded the number of zero ratings, but in 2012 and 2016, zero ratings were more numerous.

Thus, three forms of polarization – attitude constraint, the ideological separation between parties, and feelings of animosity

– have clearly increased in the United States over the last several decades. There is little evidence about changes in polarization in other nations. For Britain, Adams, Green, and Milazzo (2012) find a decline in the differences among supporters of different parties since the 1980s, but little change in attitude constraint or the frequency of "extreme" opinions on individual issues. Iyengar, Sood, and Lelkes (2012) find that there was some increase in negative feelings about the other party between 1960 and 2008, as measured by questions about whether they are "intelligent" or "selfish," but it was considerably smaller than the increase in the United States. There are many anecdotal accounts of animosity between supporters and opponents of membership in the European Union since the "Brexit" vote in June 2016. Hobolt, Leeper, and Tilley (2018) find no significant change between 2016 and 2018, but a good deal of negative feeling throughout the period.

Explanations of the Rise in Polarization

There are several possible explanations for the increase in polarization in the United States. One is that change in communications technology, especially the expansion of media choices and the growth of social media, has made it possible for people to seek out news sources that share political points of view and to restrict their discussion of politics to those who agree with them. In face-to-face communities such as neighbors or groups of co-workers, people will usually encounter some range of opinions, and since there is a continuing relationship among members of the community, there is an incentive to treat each other's opinions with respect. With online groups, those who disagree with the majority view can be excluded – even if they are not, they are likely to withdraw and try to find a more congenial community. Moreover, people seem to be more likely to express anger and hostility online than face-to-face. As a result, political discussions on social media are frequently acrimonious, involving expressions of anger and indignation against those who disagree rather than attempts to find common ground.

On the other hand, there are reasons to think that changes in communications technology potentially make people more tolerant. Social media make it possible for people to remain in touch with a wider range of people, such as old schoolmates, distant relatives, and friends of friends, giving them exposure to a wider range of opinions than they would otherwise have. Social media also make it easier to explore new ideas. In face-to-face conversation, people usually try to avoid areas of disagreement, but if an acquaintance posts an article on some controversial topic, it is possible to start reading it and stop whenever you want. As a result, people may gain more understanding of other points of view, or at least get more sense of the diversity of opinions among their family and friends. Moreover, despite the growth of social media, most people still get the bulk of their news from television and newspapers (Gentzkow 2016).

A second possibility is that the increase in polarization is the result of more general social changes. Observers such as Bishop (2009) and Murray (2012) argue that people are increasingly able to "sort" themselves so that they have less contact with people who do not share their views. Economic growth gives people more choices about what kind of work to do, where to live, and how to spend their leisure time. People generally prefer to associate with others who share their tastes and values, so the result of increased choice is that people will live in more homogeneous environments. In this analysis, increased political polarization is just one example of a general increase in the social distance among different types of people.

A third change that has been proposed as a cause of polarization is a decline of traditional communities based on place, religion, or ethnicity. In this view, people are attracted to political causes as a substitute for the sense of connection and purpose that they used to obtain from these communities. Many discussions of contemporary politics refer to "tribalism," and suggest that contemporary political disagreements are primarily about identity rather than opinions (e.g. Fukuyama 2018). Some suggest that people are particularly attracted to causes that make absolute moral claims, rather than ones that seek practical goals. For example, Sullivan

(2018) asserts that a decline of religious faith leads to "illiberal politics. The need for meaning hasn't gone away, but . . . this yearning looks to politics for satisfaction. And religious impulses . . . find expression in various political cults . . . like almost all new cultish impulses, they demand a total and immediate commitment to save the world."

An alternative view is that political polarization in the public results from polarization among political elites, partly a result of the direct transmission of views and partly because polarization among political elites leads to more frequent and intense conflict. Political conflict gives supporters of both parties a sense of grievance against the other party. For example, hearings for Supreme Court nominees have become more contentious since the 1980s, and both Democrats and Republicans can point to cases in which they believe their nominees have been treated unfairly. Grievances lead to retaliation, producing a further escalation of conflict.

Research on the Rise in Polarization

The hypothesis that a general increase in "sorting" is the underlying cause of polarization suggests that differences of opinion will increase for education and economic status, as well as for party identification. That is, if there is less contact across class lines, the opinions of different classes will diverge. It also implies that all kinds of opinions will diverge, not just political opinions – as groups have less contact with each other, they will drift apart in all respects. Desmet and Wacziarg (2018) examine group differences on all opinion questions included in the General Social Survey since the 1970s. They find that opinion differences between Democrats and Republicans are substantially higher than they were in the 1970s, but that opinion differences among the other groups that they consider – including those defined by education, ethnicity, family income, and religion – have stayed about the same or declined. Thus, there is not a general divergence of opinion among social groups – if anything, there has been some convergence.

Desmet and Wacziarg (2018) also find that opinion differences between supporters of different parties declined from the early 1970s to the late 1980s, and did not surpass the level of the early 1970s until about 2005. The timing of the increase is consistent with the idea that communications technology was the major cause of increased polarization: Fox News was established in 1996, and the internet did not become an important news source until the twenty-first century. However, Boxell, Gentzkow, and Shapiro (2017) find that polarization has increased more rapidly among older people, who are less likely to make use of the internet and social media. Older people tend to be more strongly attached to political parties, so the increase is consistent with the idea that partisans are following the leaders of their parties.

The most direct evidence is provided by Adams, Green, and Milazzo (2012) who examine polarization in British public opinion since the 1980s. During this time, Britain has experienced the same general social changes that the United States has, but the ideological difference between the leaders of the major parties has declined rather than increased. Therefore, if the increase in polarization in the United States is the results of general social changes, there should be a parallel increase in Britain; if it is the result of the public following elites, there should be a decline. In fact, they find some decline in polarization, suggesting that the growth in partisan polarization in the United States is mostly the result of the influence of political elites on their followers.

To say that a growth in polarization among political elites is the cause of polarization in the general public raises the question of why political elites have become more polarized. The prevailing view, dating back to Michels (1915), has been that democratic politics leads to a decline in polarization among political elites. One reason is the need to appeal to voters in the middle of the ideological spectrum, especially in a two-party system (Downs 1957). Another reason is experience in government: radical parties often find that some of their proposals are impractical and have to lower the expectations of their followers. This analysis implies that increases in polarization will come from outside the party system, from movements such as socialism in the nineteenth century and feminism, environmentalism, and gay rights in the 1960s and 1970s. It suggests that polarization will increase as a result of the appearance of new issues, but then decline as those issues are accommodated by the political system. This possibility will be discussed in more detail in Chapter 6.

Dimensions of Ideology

The left–right spectrum provides a reasonably accurate description of the position of most political parties, but in the general public there are two distinct dimensions of ideology, roughly corresponding to what are commonly called "economic" and "social" issues. It is possible to distinguish additional dimensions, such as foreign policy, or to divide social and economic opinions into subgroups, such as redistribution and attitudes to labor unions. However, a division into two dimensions is useful because it can be applied widely, while the additional dimensions are more specific to time and place.

There is an association among opinions on different topics within each group: for example, a person who favors an increase in the minimum wage is likely to have a positive view of labor unions, and a person who thinks that abortion should be legal is likely to think that same-sex marriage should be recognized by law. The association between opinions on issues in different groups is much weaker, and often near zero. That is, there are many people who are liberal on economic issues and conservative on social issues, or conservative on economic issues and liberal on social issues. This general point became clear soon after the first surveys of public opinion were conducted.

In one of the earliest discussions, Berelson, Lazarsfeld, and McPhee (1954, p. 184) distinguished between "position" and "style" issues. Position issues involved "matters of money and material power," and "self-interest of a relatively direct kind." Style issues involved "matters of style, taste, way of life (i.e. cultural and personal interests)" and "self-expression of a rather indirect, projective kind." They proposed that opinions on position issues differed by class, region, and industry, while opinions

71

on style issues differed among "religious and ethnic groups, cities versus country, and similar cultural groups, as well as opposing personality types." They also suggested that position and style issues had different causes: position issues "are more likely to arise out of socioeconomic conditions ... political parties can only take a stand with reference to them, whereas they can more often 'invent' the issues that are associated with Style" (Berelson, Lazarsfeld, and McPhee 1954, pp. 184–5).

There have been many other attempts to characterize the dimensions. Eysenck (1972) called the first dimension "radicalism/conservatism" and the second "tough-mindedness/tendermindedness." Hofstadter (1955, p. 84) distinguished between "interest politics, the clash of material aims and needs ... and status politics, the clash of various projective rationalizations arising from status aspirations and other personal motives." Later he concluded that the term "status" was too narrow: "if we were to speak of 'cultural politics' we might supply part of what is missing ... there have always been certain types of cultural issues, questions of faith and morals, tone and style, freedom and coercion" (Hofstadter 1962, p. 99). The efforts have continued to the present: for example, Hetherington and Weiler (2009) called the second dimension "authoritarianism," and more recently re-labeled it as "fixed" versus "fluid" (Hetherington and Weiler 2018).

The conventional terminology of "economic" and "social" issues and many of the other characterizations imply that the second dimension does not involve material interests. Häusermann and Kriesi (2015, p. 202) propose a different view, in which the second dimension mixes material and "cultural" elements: "issues such as welfare chauvinism, the unequal effects of welfare states on men and women, or the distributive balance between labor market insiders and outsiders have a clear distributive relevance, but they also relate to (more culturally connoted) considerations." They call this ideological dimension "universalism" versus "particularism": universalists hold that government programs should treat all kinds of people equally, while particularists hold that they should be targeted toward specific kinds of people or ways of life. For example, a particularist might want programs that favor native citizens over immigrants, or married couples with children over single parents. One might say that the first dimension involves the question of how much the government should intervene in the economy; the second dimension involves the nature of any intervention.

Häusermann and Kriesi (2015, p. 202) also propose that the lines between the two kinds of issues can change, and that "the boundaries between distributional (economic) and identity-based (cultural) conflicts have become increasingly blurred." Many questions could be regarded as economic issues, social issues, or something in between. For example, some people defend restrictions on immigration on the grounds that they improve the material welfare of the working class. At the same time, opinions on immigration are connected to feelings about ethnicity and national culture, apart from any economic impact (Card, Dustmann, and Preston 2012). On the other side, even issues that have been regarded as purely economic may have a "cultural" element. Traditionally, opinions on programs that redistribute income have been treated as a straightforward reflection of self-interest. For example, Campbell, Converse, Miller, and Stokes (1960, p. 205) said that "the pattern of responses to our domestic issues is best understood if we discard our notions of ideology and think rather in terms of primitive self-interest," and Kitschelt and Rehm (2019, p. 429) propose that they can be explained by "standard economic theory." However, relatively little government spending involves direct transfers between people with high and low incomes: most of it benefits various kinds of people who are regarded as deserving: for example, the elderly, people suffering from illness, low-paid workers, or mothers with dependent children. This fact suggests that support for redistributive programs involves beliefs about fairness and desert, rather than a straightforward calculation of self-interest (Barry 1990).

Influences on Social and Economic Opinions

Table 3.1 illustrates some important points about the two dimensions of ideology using correlations among variables from the

Table 3.1 Correlations Involving Selected Social and Economic Opinions

	Education	Income	Urban	Religion	Abortion	Communist	Sick	Equalize
Education	1.00							
Income	0.40	1.00						
Urban	−0.12	−0.06	1.00					
Religion	0.06	0.02	−0.06	1.00				
Abortion	**−0.19**	**−0.15**	**−0.12**	**0.30**	**1.00**			
Communist	**−0.28**	**−0.18**	**−0.11**	**0.12**	**0.20**	**1.00**		
Sick	*0.06*	*0.12*	*−0.06*	*0.10*	*0.06*	*−0.03*	*1.00*	
Equalize	*0.14*	*0.20*	*0.00*	*0.06*	*−0.01*	*−0.12*	*0.35*	*1.00*

Source: General Social Survey
N=12,589

General Social Survey. The table includes four opinion variables, which are: whether a pregnant woman who is single and does not want to marry should be able to get an abortion; whether a Communist should be allowed to give a public speech in the community; whether the government should help people pay for medical bills or people should be responsible for taking care of their own expenses; whether the government should try to reduce differences of income. The first two would generally be regarded as social issues, and the third and fourth as economic issues. To aid in distinguishing the two types of opinions, the correlations involving the two social issues are in boldface while the correlations involving the two economic issues are in italics. All variables are coded so that higher values represent a conservative opinion – opposition to abortion and allowing a Communist to speak, and belief that people should be responsible for their medical expenses and that the government should not concern itself with income differences. The table also includes education, family income, urban residence, and frequency of attendance at religious services.

There is a positive correlation (0.35) between opinions on the two economic issues – that is, people tend to be conservative on both or liberal on both. This correlation is easy to understand, since both questions involve government aid to people who are in need, but there is also a positive correlation (0.2) between opinions on the two social issues, although on the face of it they seem to have little in common with each other. The correlations between opinions on different types of issues are smaller than the correlations within each group, and the largest one is in the "wrong" direction: people who take a conservative position on the right of a Communist to speak are somewhat more likely to take a liberal position on government action income differences.

Income and education have positive correlations with opinions on the two economic issues, income redistribution and government help with medical expenses, and the correlations with income are larger than those with education. For the two social issues, the correlations with income and education are negative, meaning that more-educated and affluent people tend to be more liberal. The correlations with education are larger than those with income. People who live in urban areas have more liberal opinions on all questions, and people who attend religious services more frequently are more conservative on all, but both residence and religious observance have stronger correlations with opinions on the two social issues than with the two economic issues.

Although this example includes only a small number of opinions, it illustrates the key features of the general pattern. First, opinions on economic issues have little connection to opinions on social issues: that is, there is no tendency for people who are conservative on economic issues to be conservative on social issues. Second, people with higher social standing tend to be more conservative on economic issues, but more liberal on social issues. Third, people who live in rural areas and more religious people tend to be more conservative, especially on social issues. Finally, education is more closely connected to opinions on social issues, while income is more closely connected to opinions on economic issues. If we compare people with the same amounts of education, income makes little difference to opinions on social issues, and if we compare people with the same incomes, education makes little difference to opinions on economic issues. However, because people with more education tend to receive higher incomes, as a general rule people in "higher" social positions are more conservative on economic issues and more liberal on social issues.

Influences on the Relative Importance of the Dimensions

As discussed in Chapter 2, there has been a long-term shift in the relationship between education and party choice: educated people have moved from the right to the left. There are also short-term changes in the relationship: for example, between 2012 and 2016, the Republicans gained support among voters without a college degree and lost support among people with a college degree. Because education is associated with more liberal opinions on the "social" or "cultural" dimension of ideology, changes in the effects of education may be the result of changes in the importance of this dimension. That is, to the extent that people take "social issues" into account when voting, more-educated people will be more likely to support parties of the left. This point raises a question of whether there are any general principles that help to explain the relative importance of the two dimensions of ideology.

One plausible hypothesis is that the relative importance of the two types of issues will depend on economic conditions: in times of hardship, people will focus on economic issues, and in times of prosperity, they will turn their attention to social issues. Berelson, Lazarsfeld, and McPhee (1954, p. 185) point to the prohibition of alcohol as an example: it was a major issue during the 1920s, but was largely forgotten in the 1930s, "when there were 'more real' issues at stake." In the prosperous 1950s, economic issues seemed to recede while social issues became more prominent. Hofstadter (1955, pp. 84–5) observed that "[t]he two periods in our recent history in which status politics has been particularly important, the present era and the 1920s, have both been eras of prosperity," and proposed a general rule: "In times of depression and economic discontent . . . politics is more clearly a matter of interests . . . [i]n times of prosperity . . . status considerations among the masses can become much more important . . ." The experience of the 1960s seemed to support this view, as a variety of social issues received more attention, including the civil rights for blacks, gender equality, gay and lesbian rights, and environmentalism. However, more recent experience does not seem to fit this pattern – social issues have continued to be prominent since that time, regardless of economic conditions.

Inglehart (1977; 1990) used the same general principle to develop a model of long-term change in political alignments. He proposed that the material conditions that people experience in their youth will have a lasting effect on their priorities: people who grow up poor will develop an overriding concern with economic issues, while people who grow up in affluence will pay more attention to social issues. Continued economic growth means that, with rare exceptions, each successive generation grows up in more affluent circumstances than the previous one. As a result, social issues will gradually become more important relative to economic ones. Inglehart's model is consistent with the continued prominence of social issues since the 1960s, but is hard to square with the history of the nineteenth and early twentieth centuries. Although we do not have information from surveys, historical evidence suggests that at that time social issues were important in both American and European politics, with examples including Prohibition, women's suffrage, ethnicity, and conflicts over religion. By the middle of the twentieth century, these issues faded and economic issues became dominant. This was the time that modern public opinion research was beginning, so it is understandable that researchers took the primacy of economics as normal, but in a longer view it seems to be unusual.

A question about satisfaction with one's own financial situation was included in the American National Election Studies in 1956 and 1960 and has been repeated the General Social Survey since 1972. The highest level of satisfaction was in 1956, the first year that the question was asked; over the whole period, there has been a small downward trend. This point suggests that people's sense of what they need adjusts to recent experience – when people have more, they feel like they need more – so that economic growth does not lead to a general decline of concern with material interests. To summarize, despite the plausibility of the idea that prosperity will increase the importance of social issues, there is not much evidence to support it.

A second hypothesis is that social issues become more important in response to "status threat." When the dominant cultural traditions seem to be threatened, people will mobilize in support of them, making them more politically consequential. The threat could be the result of a direct challenge, as in the 1960s, or of more general social trends. For example, Mutz (2018) sees anxiety over the relative demographic decline of non-Hispanic whites as an important factor in the American presidential election of 2016. Although this idea seems appealing in principle, the challenge is to identify variations in "status threat." At any given time, it is possible to point to developments that some people might regard as threats to tradition. Moreover, these developments are often gradual: for example, the demographic decline of non-Hispanic whites has been going on for decades, so it is not clear why it should have been more important in 2016 than in previous elections.

A third hypothesis is that the importance of the dimensions varies depending on the activity of political and social movements. The "social" dimension may be more susceptible to this influence, since many social issues rise and fall rather than persisting. The major economic issues of today are not very different from those of 1950: examples include the level of government spending, the progressivity of taxes, and the regulation of business. The leading social issues, however, are quite different – some that were important in the 1950s, such as domestic communism, have been forgotten, and completely new ones such as gay and lesbian rights have arisen. Even when the same general area remains prominent, the specific issues have changed: for example, controversies over race have moved from legal segregation and discrimination to affirmative action and multiculturalism. Berelson, Lazarsfeld, and McPhee (1954, pp. 184) noted that "style" issues seemed to change quickly and characterized them as "short range, reference to present." Their discussion implied that that these issues were ultimately less important than economic issues – that they would not become the basis of lasting divisions. However, subsequent history suggests that the second dimension has some continuity even though the specific issues change. That is, the people who take liberal positions on one social issue are likely to take liberal positions on a new one when it arises.

What could account for the difference in persistence of social and economic issues? The basic conflicts over economics are never really resolved – the question of whether the government should try to reduce the level of inequality is always present. Moreover, changes in economic conditions mean that governments are regularly confronted with the same issues: for example, how to respond to a recession or whether to help people who have lost their jobs as a result of technological change. Social issues, in contrast, may be settled in a way that becomes more or less a matter of consensus. For example, whether it should be illegal to discriminate on the basis of race was a controversial issue in the 1950s and early 1960s – there were people who were personally opposed to discrimination but said that a law against it would be a violation of individual rights. However, after the passage of the Civil Rights Act, laws against discrimination came to be almost universally accepted. This kind of resolution does not happen with all social issues – for example, the conflict over abortion has continued for fifty years, and shows no signs of disappearing – but it happens fairly often.

Two Lefts and Two Rights?

In the general public, there are many people who are to the left on economics and the right on social issues, or to the left on social issues and the right on economics. However, electoral politics is dominated by a single dimension: with rare exceptions, parties are on the right on both types of issues, or on the left on both. Lipset (1960, pp. 121–3) argued that this pattern was the result of history: in the nineteenth and early twentieth centuries, working-class movements worked for civil rights because they were subject to oppression and sought allies among other marginalized groups. When he wrote, economic issues were more important, so there was little reason to depart from this tradition. However, as social issues have become more prominent, it seems that there is a market for parties or politicians who offer a combination of left on economic issues and right on social issues ("populist"), or right on economic issues and left on social issues ("libertarian"). In fact, it could be argued that a populist versus libertarian alignment would be more natural than the traditional one, since fewer people would face a dilemma as a result of conflicting influences from income and education – the upper classes would support parties that were to the right on economic issues and to the left on social issues, and the lower classes would support parties that were to the left on economics and to the right on social issues. However, there has been no general shift in alignments. Häusermann and Kriesi (2015, pp. 220–1) consider a number of European nations and find that the ideological basis of support for different parties continues to follow the right–left dimension. In particular, supporters of "populist" parties that get most of their support from the working class tend to take right-wing positions on both economic and social issues.

There are two possible reasons for the persistence of a general left–right dimension. One involves history – once a pattern is established, it is easier to keep old supporters than to gain new ones. If a party tried to make a shift – for example, a social democratic party began taking conservative positions on social issues – some of its traditional voters would be upset, while potential supporters might not believe that it had really changed. As a result, parties will have an incentive to preserve their base rather than to try to move in a new direction. Even new parties may benefit from having a familiar position, so that they can focus on winning voters away from one party rather than building an entirely new coalition.

A second possibility is that the left versus right dimension has some psychological basis. There have been a number of arguments along these lines, all holding that the underlying issue involves sympathy for marginalized people versus support for rules and authority (e.g. Lakoff 1996; Pratto et al. 1994). As Krugman (2019) puts it, "advocating economic inclusion seems to spill over into advocacy of racial and social inclusion, too." These analyses suggest that people who give more thought to politics will tend to be liberal on both types of issues, or conservative on both. As a result, the "populist" and "libertarian" positions will lack effective leaders and advocates, which will prevent them from being a serious political force.

The difficulty in evaluating this hypothesis is that people who are interested in politics are more likely to reflect the alignment that exists among the political parties. That is, a correlation between economic and social opinions among more people who are more interested and informed could be the result of the correlation among political leaders rather than its cause. One possible avenue of investigation is to consider opinions that are not prominent in contemporary political debate – that is, opinions on which people have to make up their own minds rather than following party leaders. A study by Feinstein and Schickler (2008) found that during the 1930s and 1940s, although there was no clear difference between the national parties on civil rights issues, state party programs gradually diverged. Outside of the South, the Democratic state parties were considerably more liberal than the Republicans by the 1950s. That is, the divergence at the level of the states preceded rather than followed the divergence of national political elites, suggesting that the issue of civil rights was important to Democratic activists. Although this study does not offer direct evidence on general public opinion, it provides some support for the idea that there is a "natural" correlation between economic and social liberalism.

Summary and Conclusions

One important point, which has been confirmed repeatedly over the years, is that ideology is very weak in the general public. Only a small fraction of the public thinks in ideological terms: "real liberals and conservatives are ... confined to the comparatively few who are deeply and seriously engaged in political life" (Kinder and Kalmoe 2017, p. 7). Many people do not have even a basic understanding of ideological terms, and most people have a mix of liberal opinions on some issues and conservative opinions on others.

Ideology

In the United States, here has been an increase in political polarization. Political views are more closely aligned with party, and there are more negative feelings between supporters of different parties. There has also been some increase in the association among opinions on different issues. Although the evidence is not definitive, it seems that these changes are primarily the result of people following political elites, rather than political elites following the public.

To the extent that ideology is present in the general public, it involves two distinct dimensions, which are often labeled "economic" and "social" issues in popular discussion. This pattern raises additional questions: how to explain changes in the importance of economic and social issues, and why political parties continue to be aligned on one left–right dimension, leaving people who combine economic liberalism with social conservatism or social liberalism with economic conservatism largely unrepresented. Another question is whether the lines between the two types of issues are changing over time or differ among nations: is the basic structure of opinions the same, or are there questions that are sometimes "social issues" and sometimes "economic issues"? If so, what factors influence their position?

4

Short-Term Change in Public Opinion

This chapter considers change in public opinion, focusing on changes in the population as a whole rather than individual change. It begins by discussing factors that affect year-to-year changes, and then turns to considering trends over the time that survey data are available.

Individual and Aggregate Change

Any individual's opinions are affected by many factors which are specific to that person and may change quickly – for example, in the space of a few years, someone might move to a new place, get a new job, get married, and have children. These experiences could affect that person's opinion on a large number of topics. Moreover, as discussed in Chapter 1, most people do not have fixed positions on most issues, so their answers to survey questions can be affected by recent news or experience, or even by information provided in the survey. For example, a person might favor the death penalty after reading about a brutal crime, but switch to opposition after reading about someone on death row who was found to have been wrongly convicted. Research has found that individual opinions on most topics are not very stable – if people are asked the same questions at a later time, many of them will give different answers (Converse 1964; Converse and Markus 1979).

In the population as a whole, however, these individual influences tend to cancel each other out. At any time, some people are getting married and others are getting divorced, some are finding jobs and others are losing jobs, some are moving to cities and others are moving to the countryside. Consequently, year-to-year changes in overall public opinion are usually small, despite the variability of individual opinions. For example, the General Social Survey includes a question on whether "you favor or oppose a law which would require a person to obtain a police permit before he or she could buy a gun?" In the five surveys taken between 2010 and 2018, support for the requirement never fell below 71 percent or rose above 75 percent, and these differences may have been merely the result of sampling variation.

Although short-term changes in public opinion are usually small, historical events can sometimes produce large shifts in a short period of time. For example, in 1978, 29 percent of Americans said the nation was spending too little on "military, armaments, and defense." Two years later, 61 percent said the nation was spending too little, presumably because of events including the Iran hostage crisis and the Soviet invasion of Afghanistan. Usually such changes are short-lived: for example, in 1982 opinions were almost back to where they had been in 1978: 32 percent said that we were spending too little on the military. However, a few historical events seem to have had a permanent, or at least a very long-lasting, effect on opinions. Before the Second World War, most Americans appeared to believe that the nation should generally stay out of international conflicts and did not need a large military except in times of war. Since the war, most Americans have believed that that the United States should be involved in international affairs and should maintain a large peacetime military force. Only a few surveys asked general questions on foreign affairs before the war, but some evidence of the change in outlook can be seen from questions about whether the United States should have joined the League of Nations: in July 1941, opinion was evenly divided, but by June 1944 53 percent said that we should have and only 20 percent said that we should not (Cantril 1951, p. 403). A large majority favored joining the United Nations, and since that time, a large majority have supported continued membership.

Factors Affecting Aggregate Change

Many different factors can influence public opinion, but research suggests that there are two general principles which apply widely. The first is that when a problem gets worse, people support more vigorous action to do something about it. Of course, there are always a number of possible ways to address a problem, but often one of them is the most straightforward and direct. For example, when crime increases, support for "get tough" policies increases; when the nation faces a foreign threat, support for defense spending increases. Figure 4.1 gives an example of this pattern: it shows the homicide rate and the percent who favored the death penalty from 1974 to 2018. The sustained high level of homicide in the 1970s and 1980s was accompanied by a rise in support for the death penalty, and the decline in the homicide rate after the early 1990s was followed by a decline in support for the death penalty. Whether or not the use of the death penalty actually reduces crime,

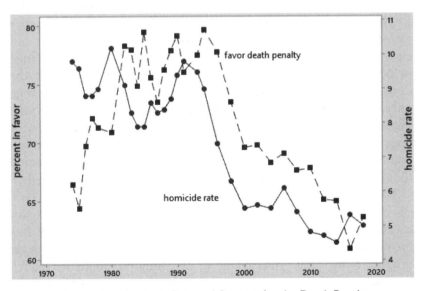

Figure 4.1 Homicide Rate and Support for the Death Penalty

Source: compiled with data from the General Social Survey and Bureau of Justice Statistics

these changes can be regarded as "rational" in the sense that they are understandable reactions to actual conditions (Page and Shapiro 1992). That is, support for the death penalty did not rise and fall suddenly in response to political campaigns or sensational stories in the media; instead, it changed gradually in response to changes in the crime rate.

The second principle is that, on many issues, opinions tend to move *against* the direction of policy favored by the governing party. Public opinion is generally more conservative when the president is a Democrat, and more liberal when the president is a Republican (Erikson, MacKuen, and Stimson 2002). This has been called a "thermostatic" reaction: just as a thermostat works to limit the range of the temperature, public opinion works to limit the range of public policy (Wlezien 1995).

The tendency to swing against the party in power is strongest for questions that involve comparisons to current policy: for example, whether the government is spending too much, too little, or about the right amount on various programs. Opinions generally shift in the direction of "spending too little" on domestic programs under Republican administrations and "spending too much" under Democratic administrations. With questions of this type, it is not clear if the change in responses should be regarded as a real change in opinion. One could say that underlying opinions about the desired level of spending remain the same and that answers change only because of a change in the standard of comparison: when the government increases the level of spending (or people think that it does), then some people who regarded the old level as too low will regard the new level as about right, and some people who regarded the old level as about right will regard the new level as too high.

The tendency to swing against the government also occurs on some questions which do not involve an explicit comparison to current policy. For example, the General Social Survey has included a question asking people to place their views on a scale ranging from "the government in Washington ought to reduce the income differences between the rich and the poor" to "the government should not concern itself" with the issue twenty-four times between 1973 and 2018. The seven years in which average opinions were most conservative – that is, in the direction of "should not concern itself" – all occurred under a Democratic president, while the three years in which opinions were most liberal occurred under a Republican.

One possible explanation for this pattern is that people implicitly use what the government is doing, or perceived to be doing, as a standard of comparison, even if it is not explicitly mentioned. For example, in the question about reducing income differences, some people might treat the current policy of the government as the midpoint of the scale. Another possible explanation is that support for a general goal is normally higher than support for any specific policy to achieve that goal. Any policy will be open to objections that it will not achieve its purpose or will have some negative side effects. Moreover, once the government seems likely to act, opponents will have reason to mobilize against it and publicize their arguments. As a result, someone who agrees that the "government should do more" when there is no immediate prospect of action might become more doubtful when definite proposals are under consideration. For example, the general idea of making sure that all people have health insurance is popular, but when Bill Clinton and Barack Obama tried to establish programs to achieve this goal, they met vigorous opposition and their proposals lost popular support (see Skocpol 1996 for a study of the response to Clinton's effort).

This interpretation suggests that public opinion will have a "conservative" bias, not in the sense of left versus right, but in the sense of giving the benefit of the doubt to the status quo. A bias of this kind would help to explain the well-known tendency for the party of the president to lose Congressional seats in mid-term elections.

Economic Conditions and Public Opinion

It is generally agreed that the state of the economy is an important influence on public opinion, but there is disagreement about the nature of that effect. One view is that during periods of prosperity, people are likely to regard poverty and unemployment as the result of individual failings but, during periods of recession, they will see them as general economic problems. As a result, support for government aid to the poor and unemployed will be higher during recessions. However, some observers argue that economic downturns reduce support for aid to the poor (Kuziemko and Norton 2011). Even during a recession, most people have jobs, so support for programs to help the poor and unemployed is primarily a matter of altruism rather than self-interest. When times are hard, people are less likely to feel that they can afford to pay taxes to support these programs.

It is possible to cite historical examples on each side of this issue. During the Great Depression of the 1930s, there were moves to the left in some nations, including the United States and Sweden, but conservative governments were elected and re-elected in other nations such as Great Britain (Friedman 2005). American public opinion was relatively liberal during the prosperous 1960s and moved to the right when inflation and unemployment increased in the 1970s (Stimson 1991). Although there is less systematic evidence, several European nations seem to have followed the same course. In Britain, for example, opinions about labor unions grew increasingly negative during the 1970s. More recently, the reaction to the recession of 2008–2009 seems to have differed among nations: the United States elected a Democratic president and Congress in 2008, but then there was a strong counter-movement and the Republicans gained a Congressional majority in 2010; Britain turned out a Labour government in 2010 and replaced it with a Conservative one; Germany kept a conservative government throughout the recession. Berman and Bartels (2014, p. 3) review the experience of a number of countries, and conclude that there was no general tendency to shift to the left or the right: their main conclusion is that "in most countries, popular reactions to the Great Recession were surprisingly muted and moderate."

This variety of experience suggests that the effect of economic conditions on public opinion is not uniform, but can go in different directions depending on other factors. One obvious possible influence on the direction is the success of government policy – if conditions improve, people will support the government and its policies, and if conditions become worse, people will turn against them. It is clear that economic conditions affect a government's chances of re-election. For example, the United States elected a Democratic president in 1976, partly in response to recession and inflation, but when conditions failed to improve voters turned to a conservative Republican in 1980. Similarly, Britain elected a Labour government during the recession of 1974, but turned to the Conservatives as conditions deteriorated again in 1979. It is reasonable to think that opinions respond in the same way – support for the policies associated with the government will increase if conditions improve and decline if conditions become worse – although there has not been much research on this issue.

Research on the effect of economic conditions on elections has found that only very recent history matters – the past year or even less (Achen and Bartels 2016, pp. 146–76). Historical accounts, however, sometimes suggest that the success or failure of a government's economic policies can lead to a lasting change in public opinion and the images of the parties. For example, it is often said that the experience of the 1930s led Americans to associate the Democrats with prosperity and the Republicans with economic hardship, while the apparent success of the Thatcher and Reagan governments in restoring economic growth in the 1980s led to a turn against "big government." There have not, however, been any systematic studies of such long-term shifts of opinion. One reason is simply that there are not many cases of severe economic downturns or dramatic changes in government policies. Another is that it is difficult to specify definitely what should count as success or failure. For example, at the time of the 1932 presidential election, the unemployment rate was about 25 percent; at the time of the 1936 election, it was about 13 percent. One could argue that the Roosevelt administration's economic policy was successful on the grounds that it had reduced the unemployment rate, or that it was a failure on the grounds that the unemployment rate was still very high.

Another possibility is that the response to economic hardship depends on the nature of political divisions. Economic downturns produce a general sense of discontent, but that discontent may be turned against different targets. People with moderate incomes might unite with the poor and seek redistribution at the expense of the rich. On the other hand, they might try to protect their *relative* position and make sure that they are not overtaken by those below them, which would mean turning against programs that help the poor (Kuziemko and Norton 2011). One factor that might help to determine which of these possibilities occurs is whether the lower classes are divided by race, religion, or other qualities. Another is the way in which political parties and social movements talk about the issues: for example, Kuziemko and Norton (2011) suggested that the language of the Occupy Wall Street movement, which contrasted the "one percent" with the "ninety-nine percent," might help to create solidarity among people with low and moderate incomes.

Economic Inequality and Public Opinion

Since the 1970s, economic inequality – the gap between the rich and the poor – has increased in most nations, with a particularly large increase in the United States. Higher inequality means that people with low incomes have more to gain from redistribution while people with high incomes have more to lose. Therefore, a straightforward analysis based on self-interest suggests high-income people will become more strongly opposed to redistribution and low-income people will become more favorable, so that class differences in opinions about redistribution will increase. The distribution of income is highly skewed – a small number of people earn far more than the average person. As a result, the number of people who could expect to gain from egalitarian redistribution is larger than the number who could expect to lose, so this analysis implies that greater inequality will also produce higher overall support for redistribution (Meltzer and Richard 1981).

Another analysis is also based on self-interest but distinguishes between different types of redistribution. Most social programs give benefits based on factors other than income: for example, they may help students, homeowners, or parents of young children. Self-interest suggests that people will support programs that help themselves or their families, or might do so in the future, but not those that help other people. Wilkinson and Pickett (2017) propose that inequality reduces the general sense of community and sympathy for others, suggesting that a rise in inequality will increase the influence of self-interest on opinions. Because most people have moderate incomes, an increase in the influence of self-interest would favor people with middle incomes at the expense of both rich and poor: support for higher taxes on the rich would increase, support for aid to the poor would decline, and support for programs that help the middle class would increase (Stigler 1970). In effect, the middle class would favor shifting the costs of government toward the rich, and the benefits toward themselves.

McCall and Kenworthy (2009) examined changes in opinions about redistribution during the period of rising inequality that began in the 1970s. They found an increase in support for the general principle of aid to the poor and for a number of social programs including education and health care, but a decline in support for increasing taxes on people with high incomes. The Gallup poll provides more detailed information regarding opinions on taxes. Since the 1990s it has regularly asked whether upper-income people pay too much, too little, or about the right amount in taxes, and the percent who say "too little" has declined despite the increase in inequality and decline in top tax rates (Newport 2016). Thus, the nature of the change was not what would have been expected from either of the analyses based on self-interest: people became more willing to help the poor, but did not turn against the rich. Class differences in opinion on these topics appear to have remained about the same or declined somewhat. On the whole, public opinion on issues related to redistribution has not changed very much over the last forty years, despite the dramatic increase in inequality.

The stability of public opinion concerning redistribution suggests that people may simply have not been very conscious of the increase in inequality, particularly the rise of top incomes. Some surveys have asked people to estimate the earnings of people in various occupations and found that most people substantially underestimate the earnings of corporate executives (Weakliem and Biggert 2013). Norton and Ariely (2011) asked respondents to give estimates of the general level of inequality in the United States, and found that most estimates were far lower than the actual levels. This lack of awareness many reflect a general psychological tendency to focus on one's immediate surroundings. A person is likely to be more upset if they are paid slightly less than someone who does the same kind of work than if they are paid much less than someone who does a very different kind of work. Runciman (1966) found that when asked about the kinds of people who earned more than they deserved, people usually offered examples from approximately their own social standing. Another possibility is that the lack of awareness reflects a lack of media coverage of top incomes. Although the general issue of economic inequality has received a good deal of attention in recent years, the exact incomes of wealthy people are not commonly reported, except for unrepresentative cases such as professional athletes.

Bartels (2005) suggests that a focus on one's immediate sur- roundings helps to explain popular support for the 2001 and 2003 tax cuts proposed by George W. Bush. The proposal was broadly popular although most of the benefits went to a people with high incomes. Bartels argued that people supported the tax cuts "not because they were indifferent to economic inequality, but because they largely failed to connect inequality and public policy." People who thought that they paid too much in taxes tended to support the tax cuts, regardless of their views about inequality. Bartels (2005, p. 21) labeled the dominant pattern as "unenlightened self-interest": in his view, people focused on the immediate benefit to themselves and ignored the larger implications of the tax cuts. On the other hand, Graetz and Shapiro (2006) point out that many people remained opposed to the inheritance tax, even when informed that the tax applied to only a small fraction of estates, or when offered proposals to raise the limit or exempt family busi- nesses. They conclude that support for repeal of the inheritance tax was based on popular ideas about fairness, particularly the right to pass property on to one's children, and that opponents of repeal were ineffective because they focused on appealing to self-interest rather than countering the moral arguments.

Another possible explanation of the pattern found by Bartels is that people lack confidence in the willingness or ability of the government to reduce inequality. Kuziemko, Norton, Saez, and Stantcheva (2015; see Kuziemko and Stantcheva 2013 for a summary) designed an online survey that provided a randomly selected fraction of their sample with a "tutorial" on trends in economic inequality. They found that respondents who were exposed to the information were more likely to agree that inequality was a serious problem, but less likely to agree that the government could be trusted at least some of the time. That is, rather than concluding that the government should do more, people seem to have concluded that the government was unable or unwilling to do anything. Weakliem and Biggert (2013, p. 83) observe that, whenever a major tax reform has been considered, most people have said that most of the benefits would go to the rich, regardless of the specific features of the reform. These points suggest that people may not pay much attention to changes in top tax rates because they assume that the rich will find a way to turn any reform to their advantage. In effect, they focus on their own taxes because that is all that they are sure about.

Parallel Publics

Page and Shapiro (1992) found that in the short term changes in opinions are usually about the same among all kinds of people. They called this pattern "parallel publics": when opinions are plotted against time, the lines representing different groups will be parallel. Figure 4.2 gives an example: changes in support for the death penalty among men and women between 1974 and 2018. Men were consistently more likely to support the death penalty, but the pattern of change was the same among men and women: support increased until about 1990 and then declined. Consequently, the gap in opinions between men and women remained the same throughout the period. Sometimes opinions in

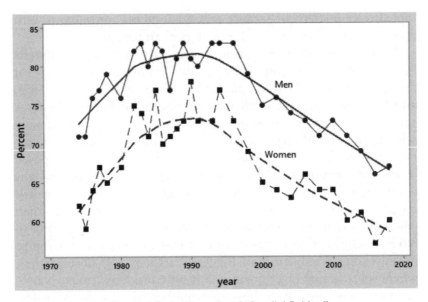

Figure 4.2 An Example of "Parallel Publics"

Source: compiled with data from General Social Survey

different groups gradually converge or diverge, but it is rare for them to move in different directions over a short period of time.

Parallel changes in opinion mean that people in different groups respond in the same way to whatever factors influence opinions. These factors might include relevant historical events or conditions or what House and Mason (1975) call the "spirit of the times" – general ideas that, for whatever reason, are prevalent at a particular time. One reason that responses tend to be similar is that many social changes affect most kinds of people in similar ways: for example, during a recession, almost all groups suffer a loss of income. A second reason is people often care about the welfare of others: for example, a person with a secure job may sympathize with people who become unemployed. A third reason is that people get much of their information from a common source, the mass media. For example, if crime is rising, even someone whose own neighborhood remains safe is likely to encounter news stories about the problem. These points mean that parallel changes in opinion can be regarded as a form of consensus, since they indicate that different groups have something in common – they receive the same information and react to it in the same way (Lipset 1960, p. 15).

Perceptions of Facts

The idea of parallel publics also applies to the perceptions of facts. Although there are often group differences in perceptions – for example, people with higher incomes tend to rate economic conditions more favorably – *changes* in perception generally move in parallel. For example, if unemployment falls, all groups will rate economic conditions more favorably. There is one important exception to this pattern: supporters of a political party evaluate conditions more favorably when their party is in power. This point means that supporters of different parties react differently to a change in party control of government. For example, in October 2008, when the Republican George W. Bush was President, 46 percent of Republicans and 80 percent of Democrats rated economic conditions as poor; in December 2009, when the Democrat Barack Obama was President, 59 percent of Republicans and only 38 percent of Democrats rated them as poor. That is, between October 2008 and December 2009 Republicans became somewhat more negative about economic conditions, while Democrats became substantially more positive. Independents fell in between, becoming somewhat more positive.

In recent years, there has been concern that the influence of partisanship on perceptions of the facts is growing (Shapiro and Bloch-Elkon 2008). References to "post-truth politics" and "post-truth society" have become common, and in 2016 the Oxford Dictionaries chose "post-truth" as their word of the year. Although there is not much systematic research on this issue, Shapiro and Bloch-Elkon (2006) provide a striking example from the Iraq war. The major argument that the United States government offered as justification for the war was that Iraq possessed "weapons of mass destruction." In June 2003, 69 percent of Democrats and 87 percent of Republicans believed that Iraq had possessed "weapons of mass destruction" before the war began. By December 2003, after no evidence of such weapons had been discovered, belief had fallen to 50 percent among Democrats, but remained at 88 percent among Republicans. That is, the failure to find weapons of mass destruction caused many Democrats to change their minds, but made no difference among Republicans. As more time passed without the discovery of weapons of mass destruction, the number who believed that Iraq had possessed them fell among Republicans, but less than it did among Democrats. As a result, the gap between the supporters of different parties continued to grow: in April 2004, only 36 percent of Democrats but 80 percent of Republicans believed that Iraq had possessed weapons of mass destruction.

This was an issue on which most people had no personal experience, and the phrase "weapons of mass destruction" was open to various interpretations. Remote and complex issues of this kind are likely to be especially sensitive to the influence of partisanship. However, even on everyday issues such as basic economic conditions, people obtain much of their information from the media rather than immediate personal experience. Therefore, perceptions may be influenced by partisanship, especially if party leaders dispute the media consensus. Enns, Kellstedt, and McAvoy (2012) found that partisan differences in the ratings of economic conditions were larger in the George W. Bush administration than they had been in previous administrations. The last year included in their analysis was 2007; given the increase in ideological polarization in the last decade, it would be interesting to see if the influence of partisanship on perceptions has continued to increase since then.

One possible reason for a growth in the influence of partisanship on perceptions is simply stronger partisanship: on disputed issues, partisans may be inclined to accept the claims of their own party leaders and reject competing views. A second reason involves changes in the news media created by the rise of the internet. There are more sources of news and opinion than there were in the past and many of them represent specific points of view, so that it is easier for people to find ones that confirm their own opinion and more difficult to distinguish reliable from unreliable sources of information. Even if people are not trying to confirm their pre-existing opinions, social media may push them in that direction by recommending stories that are similar to those that they have previously read. A third potential reason is declining confidence in institutions. For example, a person who reads a news story about the scientific consensus on climate change may remain unconvinced because he does not trust the news media, the scientific community, or both.

Trends in Public Opinion

As discussed in Chapter 1, the first opinion surveys were conducted in the 1930s, giving a record of up to eighty years of change in public opinion. This section will begin with an overview of long-term changes in opinions on a variety of topics, and then will consider the explanation of those changes.

Racial Equality

There has been a large decline in support for segregation and in open expressions of racial prejudice. For example, in 1956, only 49 percent of whites agreed that "white students and negro students should go to the same schools." Support for that position rose to 71 percent in 1968, 85 percent in 1977, and 92 percent in 1985. (Until the 1960s, surveys asked about "negroes" or "colored people"; since the 1970s, most have used "blacks" or "African Americans"). In 1958, only 37 percent said that they would vote for "a generally well-qualified man for president if he happened to be a Negro." The figure rose to 69 percent in 1969 and 95 percent in 1999. In 1963, 60 percent of whites said "yes" when asked "do you think there should be laws against marriages between negroes and whites." Support for that position fell to 31 percent in 1980 and 11 percent in 2002, the most recent year in which the question was asked. All of these changes have been

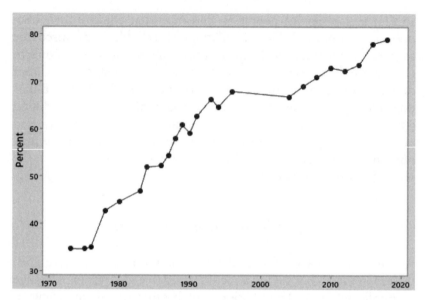

Figure 4.3 Percent in Favor of Law Against Discrimination in Home Sales

Source: compiled with data from the General Social Survey

steady and gradual – opinions have moved in the same direction over a long period of time.

There has also been an increase in support for government action against racial discrimination. The General Social Survey includes a question on a hypothetical choice between a law saying "that a homeowner can decide for himself whom to sell his house to, even if he prefers not to sell to blacks" and a law saying "that a homeowner cannot refuse to sell to someone because of their race or color." Figure 4.3 shows the changes in support for the second option, which rose from 35 percent in 1973 to 79 percent in 2018. The movement was not completely steady – for example, there seems to have been little or no change between 1993 and 2004 – but there are no periods in which support declined significantly.

There has not, however, been an increase in support for all measures to reduce racial inequality. Since the 1970s, majorities have expressed approval of "affirmative action" in principle. For example, in response to a 2019 Gallup Poll question on whether you "generally favor or oppose affirmative action programs for racial minorities," 61 percent said they favored such programs and only 30 percent were opposed. At the same time, questions about "preferences" for blacks consistently find large majorities in opposition, even when they specify that the preferences are intended to make up for past discrimination. Since 1994, the General Social Survey has asked "are you for or against preferential hiring and promotion of blacks?" after giving brief arguments on both sides of the question. Between 1994 and 2014, support for "preferential hiring and promotion" never rose above 20 percent. It has increased somewhat since that time, but even in 2018 only 24 percent said that they were in favor of preferential hiring and promotion.

There has been a vigorous debate about the interpretation of these changes. Some observers argue that, although they have become more reluctant to express prejudice directly, many or most whites are still committed to maintaining racial inequality. One way that they can express this commitment without seeming prejudiced is by asserting that America is now a "colorblind" society, so that racial inequality must be the result of "individual taste, talent and inclination" (Bobo 2017, p. S90). Another is by devising apparently race-neutral justifications for opposing measures that would reduce racial inequality: for example, saying that college admission should be based strictly on "merit" as measured by grades and test scores. Other observers hold that "political rather than racial considerations stand at the center of whites' attitudes towards racial policy" (Sears, Hetts, Sidanius, and Bobo 2000, p. 40). For example, a person who has positive feelings about blacks and thinks that racial inequality is a bad thing might nevertheless oppose some policies that would reduce racial inequality because they conflict with other principles. The papers in Sears, Sidanius, and Bobo (2000) provide an overview of the debate.

It is difficult to resolve this debate, since to a large extent it involves motives. For example, if a white person says that he opposes affirmative action because it violates the principle of equal treatment, does that reflect a real commitment to the principle or is it a rationalization of concern about protecting the racial hierarchy? Experiments can shed some light on this issue – for example, participants can be provided with different messages or information before they are asked a question. However, experiments do not provide information about historical change – they can show that concern about protecting the racial hierarchy is a factor today, but cannot show whether it is a larger or smaller factor than it was in the past.

It is clear that there are racial differences in beliefs about the amount of discrimination in contemporary society. For example, in 2013 a Pew survey asked how much discrimination against African-Americans there was: 16 percent of whites and 48 percent of blacks chose "a lot"; 39 percent of whites and only eight percent of blacks chose "only a little" or "none at all." For many years, these differences were relatively stable, but recently white opinion has shifted toward seeing more discrimination. For example, in 2015 a Kaiser survey asked the same question and found that 32 percent of whites said that there was a lot of discrimination and 23 percent said that there was only a little or none at all. It is not clear why this change occurred, but one possible cause is publicity given to police mistreatment of blacks, both in media coverage and in videos circulated on social media. Examination of a number of questions suggests that opinions began to change in late 2014 and early 2015, not long after extensive media coverage of the deaths of Michael Brown in August 2014 and Tamir Rice in November (Weakliem 2010–2019, April 20, 2019). A number of other opinions related to race have also changed – for example, there has been a substantial increase in agreement that "blacks have gotten less than they deserve" and that discrimination is the major reason for racial inequality (Yglesias 2019).

Gender and Sexuality

On gender, there has been a large move toward support for the principle of equal rights, and a corresponding decline in support for the idea that women should focus on taking care of their homes and families. In 1937, only 33 percent said that they would vote for a woman for president "if she qualified in every other respect." A slightly different question has been asked since the 1940s – "if the party whose candidate you most often support nominated a woman for President of the United States, would you vote for her if she seemed qualified for the job?" Willingness to vote for a woman rose from 48 percent in 1949 to 57 percent in 1967, 78 percent in 1984, and 95 percent in 2010. Since 1977, the General Social Survey has asked people if they agree or disagree that "it is much better for everyone involved if the man is the achiever outside the home and the woman takes care of the home and family." In 1977, 66 percent said that they agreed or strongly agreed, but the figure fell below 40 percent by 1990 and below 25 percent in 2018.

Opinions on abortion have followed a different pattern. Support for legal abortion increased from the early 1960s to the early 1970s, but has remained essentially unchanged since that time. Substantial majorities believe that abortion should be legal, but also favor "procedural and other restrictions, including waiting periods, parental consent, spousal notification, and bans on 'partial birth' abortions" (Luks and Salamone 2008, p. 101).

Questions on gays and lesbians do not go back as far as questions on race and gender. One of the first was included in the General Social Survey in 1973: whether "a man who admits he is a homosexual be allowed to teach in a college or university or not?" Opinion was evenly divided, with 47 percent saying that he should and 48 percent that he should not. Support increased steadily to 89 percent in 2018. In 1988, the General Social Survey asked whether "homosexual couples should have the right to marry one another," and only 12 percent said that they should. The question was not asked again until 2004, when 30 percent said that they should. Since that time, it has been asked regularly, and support has risen steadily to 68 percent in 2018.

There has also been a shift toward more relaxed standards on many issues of personal morality. For example, the General Social Survey has regularly asked "if a man and woman have sex relations before marriage, do you think it is always wrong, almost always wrong, wrong only sometimes, or not wrong at all?" In 1972, 36 percent said it was always wrong and 28 percent that it was not wrong at all; in 2018, only 18 percent said it was always wrong and 62 percent said that it was not wrong at all. However, the shift toward more relaxed standards has not occurred for all questions of personal morality. For example, the number who say that "a married person having sexual relations with someone other than the marriage partner" is always wrong has *increased* slightly since the 1970s.

Economic Issues

Turning to economic issues, questions on whether people approve or disapprove of labor unions have been asked since the 1930s. There was a decline in approval from about 65 to 70 percent in the early surveys to 55 to 60 percent in the late 1970s; since that time, there has been little change (Gallup 2019b). Questions on the minimum wage have been asked on many occasions since the 1940s, and almost invariably find majority support for an increase. For example, a Gallup poll from 1946 found that 65 percent were in favor of an increase from 40 cents to 65 cents an hour (about $5.50 to $9.00 in today's terms), while a PRRI/Atlantic poll from 2018 found that 63 percent were in favor of an increase from $7.25 to $15.00 per hour.

In 1939, a Roper/Fortune survey asked if "our government should or should not redistribute wealth by heavy taxes on the rich": 35 percent said that it should and 54 percent that it should not. This question was repeated by the Gallup Poll in 1998, when 45 percent said it should, and a number of times since then, most recently in 2016, when 52 percent said that it should.

A survey in 1947 asked respondents whether "the most important job for the government is to make it certain that there are good opportunities for each person to get ahead on his own" or "to guarantee every person a decent and steady job and standard of living" – 50 percent chose "provide opportunities" while 43 percent chose a guaranteed job and standard of living. Although this question has never been repeated, several similar ones have been asked in later surveys. In 1978, when offered a choice between "the government should see to it that every person has a job and a good standard of living" and "the government should let each person get ahead on his own," 33 percent favored the first option and 59 percent favored the second. In 1986, this question was asked again: 40 percent favored the first option and 54 favored the second. In 2016, a survey asked if "the government in Washington should see to it that every person has a job and a good standard of living or the best thing . . . is to get out of the way and let the free market help people succeed?" This time, 47 percent thought the government should "see to it that every person has a job and a good standard of living," and 46 percent thought it should "get out of the way." Overall, there seems to be little change in opinions on general issues of redistribution and government responsibility to provide jobs.

One economic issue on which there *has* been a trend is support for public ownership of business. In 1937, the Gallup Poll asked "Would you like to have the government own and control the banks?" 41 percent said yes, 42 percent no, with 17 percent undecided. In 2009, a CBS News survey asked exactly the same question, and only 14 percent said yes, while 76 percent said no. The Gallup Poll asked a similar question between 1945 and 1953, and support for government ownership of banks fell from 34 percent to 14 percent over that period. There have also been a number of questions about government ownership of electric power companies: support dropped in the first few years after the Second World War, and has remained about the same since then. Although questions about government ownership have been scarce in recent years, that fact may itself be evidence of the decline of public support.

Crime

On crime, opinions generally became more liberal until the late 1960s, then more conservative, and since the 1990s have been moving back in a liberal direction. Beginning in the 1930s, the Gallup Poll has asked "are you in favor of the death penalty for persons convicted of murder?" In 1937, 60 percent said they were in favor of the death penalty. Support fell gradually to 42 percent

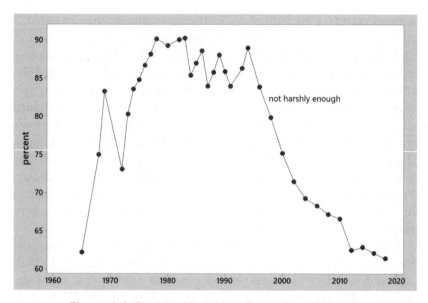

Figure 4.4 Opinions About How Courts Treat Criminals

Source: compiled with data from Gallup and General Social Survey

in 1966, and then rose to a high of 80 percent in 1994. Since then, support has declined steadily, falling to 56 percent in 2018. Since the 1960s, a question on whether "the courts in this area deal too harshly or not harshly enough with criminals" has been asked, first by the Gallup Poll and later by the General Social Survey. Figure 4.4 shows the percentage saying "not harshly enough." This rose rapidly in the 1960s and early 1970s, and stayed at about 85 percent until the mid-1990s, but since that time has fallen to the levels of the mid-1960s. Support for the "too harshly" option has increased in recent years: it reached ten percent for the first time in 2002 and rose above 20 percent in 2016 and 2018.

Freedom of Speech

Finally, support for the freedom to express unpopular opinions appears to have increased. In 1954, 89 percent said that "a man who admits he is a Communist" and teaches in a college or university should be fired from his position (Stouffer 1955). When the General Social Survey asked the same question in 1972, 64 percent said that he should be fired. That number has gradually declined to about 33 percent in 2018. There have also been questions about the right of a Communist to give a speech or have a book in a public library, and support has increased over the period. Since the 1970s, the General Social Survey has had parallel questions about "a person who advocates doing away with elections and letting the military run the country" and "a person who believes that Blacks are genetically inferior". Support for the right of someone who supports military rule to make a speech, have a book in a public library, or teach in a college has steadily increased, while support for the corresponding rights of someone who believes that blacks are inferior has stayed about the same.

Support for the right to advocate a position is influenced not only by commitment to the principle of tolerance, but also by opinions about that position – how strongly people disapprove of it and whether they see it as a serious threat. Some of the increase in willingness to allow Communists to express their opinions might reflect a decline in the perceived threat from Communism rather than an increase in support for the principle of tolerance. On the other hand, support for the belief that blacks are genetically inferior has declined since the 1970s. The fact that support for the right to advocate that position has remained constant as that position has become increasingly unpopular suggests that support for the principle of tolerance has increased. Finally, military rule has never been a serious prospect in the United States and has never had significant mainstream support, so the increase in support for the right to advocate that position can be taken as a relatively pure measure of changes in tolerance.

Summary

There have been trends continuing over more than fifty years in opinions on many, although not all, "social" issues. Almost all of the trends are in what would conventionally be considered a liberal direction. There have been no clear trends in opinions on economic issues, with the exception of a decline in support for government ownership. For issues related to crime, there was a shift in a conservative direction from the 1960s to the 1980s, but a liberal movement since the 1990s. These shifts seem to be closely related to changes in the crime rate. Thus, on the whole it appears that public opinion has moved in a liberal direction since surveys began in the 1930s.

Is there a Liberal Trend in Public Opinion?

There have been some efforts to construct a general index of public opinion by combining opinions on a variety of topics. Any question that has been asked on at least two different occasions provides some information about change in public opinion. Stimson (1991) found that, for issues which can be characterized in terms of liberal and conservative, opinions on all topics tend to move in the same direction from year to year. That is, it is possible to say that public opinion in general is more liberal or more conservative than it was in the previous year. He constructed a measure of "policy mood" going back to 1952, based primarily on "New Deal" issues involving taxing and spending, the regulation of business and labor, and social welfare programs. This was later extended into a more comprehensive index of opinion including almost 400 survey questions on a wide range of areas (Policy Agendas Project 2015).

Figure 4.5 shows estimates for both of these measures of "policy mood," with higher numbers meaning more liberal. Both estimates show the same general pattern: a liberal movement until the early 1960s, then a conservative movement until about 1980, followed by several rises and falls.

The evidence discussed in the previous section suggests that a substantial number of opinions have moved steadily in a liberal direction, while very few have moved steadily in a conservative direction (see also Smith 1990). As a result, a general index of public opinion that combines a variety of opinions should also show a trend in a liberal direction. However, the indexes calculated

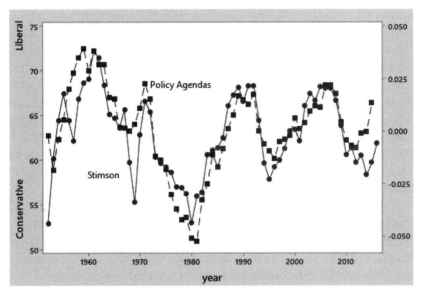

Figure 4.5 Estimates of General Public Opinion

Source: compiled with data from James A. Stimson (stimson.web.unc.edu) and Policy Agendas Project (https://www.comparativeagendas.net/us)

by Stimson and the Policy Agendas Project do not show any trend: according to both, public opinion was at its most liberal around 1960. One reason for the difference is that these indexes are limited to policy issues – that is, questions involving potential government action. As a result, some of the opinions that show the strongest trends, such as willingness to vote for a black presidential candidate, are not included. A second reason is that the questions that are asked in surveys change over time as old issues fade and new issues arise. For example, surveys did not ask about attitudes toward gays and lesbians until the 1970s, or about same-sex marriage until the 1990s. Other questions have been dropped, often because public opinion came to overwhelmingly favor one side: for example, between 1959 and 1983 a number of surveys asked "in some places in the United States it is not legal to supply birth control information. How do you feel about this – do you think birth control information should be available to anyone who wants it, or not?" During the time that the question was asked, support for the availability of birth control information rose from 73 to 90 percent. Thus, an important part of the evidence for a liberal trend in opinion is difference between the questions that are asked today and those that were asked in the past. Issues that were once so far out of the mainstream that no one thought to ask about them are now the subjects of controversy, and issues that were once controversial have become matters of consensus. An index of opinion at any time must be based on the questions that were asked at that time, so it cannot take account of these changes.

To summarize, public opinion has generally moved in a liberal direction over the past fifty years, but with significant short-term fluctuation around the trend. To use a metaphor suggested by Davis (1980), the year-to-year variation is like changes in the weather within the context of a gradually changing climate.

Backlash

The term "backlash" is widely used in discussions of politics. It first appeared in the 1960s, with reference to civil rights (Lipset 1964). In the early and mid-1960s, there seemed to be widespread public support for ending segregation, and for social reform more generally. After working for the passage of the Civil Rights Act in 1964, Lyndon Johnson won a landslide victory with over 60 percent of the popular vote, and the Democrats gained overwhelming majorities in both houses of Congress. Soon, however, the political mood seemed to change. The Democrats lost a large number of seats in the 1966 Congressional elections, and their share of the vote fell to 43 percent in the 1968 presidential election, while an independent segregationist candidate, George Wallace, won 14 percent. The victorious Republican candidate, Richard Nixon, said little about civil rights, but promised tough policies against crime and civil disorder, which some observers saw as veiled criticism of integration and civil rights protests. During his first term in office, Nixon won over many of Wallace's supporters and was re-elected by a landslide in 1972. Thus, in less than a decade, there seemed to be a dramatic shift from left to right.

The general idea of "backlash" is that rapid movement in one direction produces a reaction in the other direction, similar to the "thermostatic" model discussed earlier in this chapter. However, the term also implies a distinction between "front" and "back": that is, a prevailing direction of change, of which the "backlash" is just a temporary reversal. Consequently, the term "backlash" is almost always applied to conservative movements. As Lipset (1964, p. 23) put it "the politics of 'backlash' . . . is a consequence of the fact that the United States is becoming more liberal. The groups now reacting with such desperation are desperate precisely because they are growing less influential and less numerous." Other authors have offered similar analyses of many subsequent political movements. Recently the success of Donald Trump and the growth of various right-wing "populist" parties has been explained as a backlash against immigration and ethnic diversity (Inglehart and Norris 2016; Alexander 2019).

Although backlash seems easily visible in political history, it is hard to see in public opinion surveys. For example, opinions on questions involving race continued to move in a liberal direction during the late 1960s and early 1970s, and in recent years, attitudes to immigration have become more favorable in the United States and most nations of Western Europe, even as anti-immigrant movements have grown stronger (Fischer 2017; Dennison and Geddes 2019). This point suggests that backlash may involve a change in the relative importance of different issues – when people who object to social changes become more likely to act on their opinions, whether by voting for a candidate or joining in protests. For example, people who had been opposed to civil rights but had supported the Democrats for other reasons in 1964 might have given higher priority to civil rights in 1968, and consequently turned to the Republicans. Backlash may also involve changes in the specific issues that are the subject of attention. For example, in the late 1960s and early 1970s, courts began to mandate "busing" – sending children to schools outside of their neighborhood – in order to achieve racial integration. Many people who opposed laws mandating segregation were not in favor of busing, and politicians who had opposed integration could recast themselves as opponents of busing. Consequently, people who had previously supported liberal candidates could switch to supporting conservatives without changing their opinions on existing issues.

Changes in public opinion on general topics such as support for racial equality are usually gradual. Government policy, however, moves unevenly: long stretches when there is little change, occasionally broken by major pieces of legislation or new initiatives. Moreover, changes in government policy are generally clustered: organizations that had been pushing for change will become more confident and make additional demands, officials charged with implementing a policy may encounter unexpected problems and propose new policies to deal with them, and political leaders may believe that the tide is running in favor of change. As a result, there are periods of rapid reform. The uneven pace of change in government policy means that substantial discrepancies between public opinion and policy can appear. Backlash could be seen as the result of government policies running "ahead" of public opinion. In some cases, the backlash might fade as public opinion continues to move in the same direction. For example, in the United States, same-sex marriage became a political issue in the mid-1990s because of court decisions. At first, it was unpopular with the public, and voters or legislators in a majority of states approved constitutional amendments specifying that marriage could take place only between a man and a woman. However, as public support continued to increase, several states passed legislation recognizing same-sex marriage, and more political figures came out in favor of it. When in 2015 the Supreme Court ruled that same-sex marriage must be recognized in all states, there was little public resistance.

In other cases, backlash might fade because the government abandons or partially withdraws from unpopular policies. For example, busing was a major issue during the 1970s, but became less prominent as it was used less frequently in the 1980s and 1990s. Similarly, some forms of affirmative action were tried in the 1970s but were abandoned after meeting strong opposition, while other forms continued and came to be generally accepted.

Social Movements and Public Opinion

Like government policy, social movement activity tends to be uneven: it can appear, grow, and decline in a short period of time. For example, there was a large and active movement in favor of women's suffrage, but after the right to vote was obtained, it rapidly declined rather than moving on to other issues of gender equality. In the next few decades, public opinion seemed to move gradually in favor of gender equality; Kluckhohn (1958, p. 207) saw a "drift toward equalization of the roles of the sexes" over the previous generation. However, few if any observers seem to have anticipated the appearance of the feminist movement in the 1960s. Within the space of a few years, there were demands for immediate change in conditions that had previously been accepted as natural, such as the almost complete exclusion of women from managerial and professional occupations. The government did take some important steps – for example, the Civil Rights Act of 1964 banned discrimination by gender as well as by race – but rather than satisfying the pressure for change, those measures seemed to stimulate further demands.

Social movements can differ in goals – they may be moderate or radical – and in tactics – they may work through the electoral system, hold peaceful demonstrations, or engage in violent action. Often there are a number of different groups working for the same general end that take different approaches. This variety of social movements raises the question of how different rhetoric and actions will affect public opinion. On the one hand, "extremism" may be more effective in drawing attention to an issue. It may also help to extend the range the range of possibilities. If a proposal gets attention from politicians and the media, it has a chance of gaining popular support. Even if it remains unpopular, it may help to shift opinion. Some people may try to steer a course midway between what they see as the extremes. If this is the case, introducing a new and more extreme proposal to the debate will cause "moderate" opinion to move in the direction of that proposal. The range of possibilities is sometimes known as the "Overton Window" after the policy analyst Joseph P. Overton (1960–2003), although the idea is undoubtedly much older (Mackinac Center 2019).

For example, if a conservative party calls for a top tax rate of 30 percent and a liberal party calls for a top rate of 50 percent, moderates may favor a rate of 40 percent; if the liberal party calls for 70 percent, moderates may favor 50 percent. On the other hand, extremism may provoke a reaction if people regard a proposal as ridiculous or offensive: opponents will point to the extremists as the true representatives of the cause. For example, if the liberal party called for a top rate of 95 percent, moderates might simply reject that as unreasonable and support the conservative position.

Finally, it is possible that extreme movements can have a negative effect on public opinion in the short term, but a positive effect in the longer term. Alexander (2019, p. 5) says that change is "triggered by 'frontlash' movements, by avant-gardes whose vision is way ahead of their time . . . and whose victories . . . are experienced as profoundly threatening to vested interests." In his view, movements that push ahead of public opinion are necessary for change, even if they lead to backlash in the short run.

One general point is clear: the immediate reaction to any kind of disruption is usually negative. In May 1961, a Gallup poll asked: "Do you think 'sit-ins' at lunch counters, 'freedom buses,' and other demonstrations by Negroes will hurt or help the Negro's chances of being integrated in the South?" A majority said that they would hurt, and only 28 percent said that they would help. In June 1963, another survey asked: "Do you think mass demonstrations by negroes are more likely to help or hurt the negro's cause for racial equality?" with similar results: 27 percent said that they would help the cause and 60 percent that they would hurt it. This question was asked again in 1964, and only 16 percent said that they would help. Even when a peaceful civil rights march was attacked by police in Selma, Alabama, public opinion was divided: 48 percent said they sympathized with the demonstrators,

21 percent with the police, while the rest were undecided or did not sympathize with either side. However, when a survey in 1973 asked: "Do you feel the protest marches led by Martin Luther King in the 1960s speeded up civil rights legislation, slowed it down, or didn't make much difference one way or the other?", 67 percent said that the protests speeded up legislation, only three percent said that they slowed it down, and 23 percent said that they had not made much difference.

To summarize, in the 1960s most people said they supported the goals of the civil rights movement, but large majorities opposed even peaceful demonstrations. However, within a few years, most said that the protests had been effective. Thus, although the immediate reaction to the demonstrations was negative, the long-term reaction was positive. The explanation for this difference may be that most people did not want to think about segregation: they opposed it, but hoped that it would naturally fade away. Consequently they had a negative reaction to actions that made them confront the issue, but after the protests led to government action, they accepted the results as a good thing. Thus, even though the initial reaction was negative, the strategy of the movement was probably effective in pushing public opinion along more rapidly than it would otherwise have gone.

Like civil rights protests, demonstrations against the Vietnam War were unpopular when they took place. For example, in 1969, only about 20 percent said that they approved of public protests against the war, and about 60 percent said that protests hurt the chances of reaching a peace agreement. Although retrospective evaluations were more favorable, they were still divided: a 1973 survey found that 20 percent said the anti-war demonstrations had shortened the war, 22 percent that they had prolonged it, and 49 percent that they had not made much difference. The reason that retrospective judgments about anti-war demonstrations were less favorable than those about civil rights demonstrations may be that, although most people had come to regard the war as a mistake, they did not regard it as morally wrong.

Framing

A "frame" could be defined as a perspective on an issue, and framing as the act of offering a perspective. A simple form of framing is attaching labels to issues and positions on those issues. For example, supporters of legal abortion usually refer to themselves as "pro-choice" rather than "pro-abortion." People who are involved with an issue often feel strongly about labels, but their impact on the public is usually small. For example, in the late 1990s, opponents of the inheritance tax adopted and promoted the term "death tax," in the hope that it would make the tax seem less appealing (Graetz and Shapiro 2006). In 2003, a survey asked randomly selected halves of the sample about the "federal estate tax" and the "federal estate tax that some people call the death tax": 54 percent of those who were asked the first form and 60 percent of those who were asked the second form said that they favored abolishing it. Given the size of the sample, the difference could have been the result of sampling variations. These results suggest that the difference in labels had no more than a small impact, and that the tax was not popular under either name.

An example in which labeling may be more important is provided by two questions asked to randomly selected halves of respondents to the General Social Survey, one on "welfare" and the other on "assistance to the poor." Only about 20 percent say that we are spending too little on "welfare" and 49 percent say that we are spending too much, but 66 percent say we are spending too little on "assistance to the poor" and only ten percent say we are spending too much. Bartels (2003, p. 43) offers this difference as an example of the importance of framing: "very different mental images are attached to the same set of programs and policies." However, an alternative interpretation is that responses differ because people do not understand the questions as referring to the same programs: in popular usage, "welfare" seems to mean aid to working-age people without jobs, while "assistance to the poor" covers a wider range, including programs to help the elderly, disabled people, and the working poor, which tend to be more popular.

Even if labels make a difference for individual answers to survey questions, they may not have much influence on *changes* in overall public opinion. If different labels are available, people will use the one that is most congenial with their opinions – for example, opponents of social programs will speak of "welfare" while supporters speak of "helping the poor." That is, rather than labels influencing opinions, opinions will influence the choice of label.

Another aspect of framing is making connections among issues. Debates over political issues often involve competing claims of what a particular issue is "really about." This kind of framing will affect, not only opinions on a particular issue, but also the pattern of association among different opinions. For example, it is sometimes suggested that "welfare" is unpopular because people associate it with racial minorities. This hypothesis suggests that opinions about "welfare" should be strongly associated with opinions about racial issues. Smith (1987) investigated this issue and found that opinions about "welfare" and "assistance to the poor" had similar correlations to opinions on racial issues. However, he found that opinions about welfare had a stronger correlation with views of one's own tax burden – people who thought that they paid too much in taxes were more likely to think the nation was spending too much on welfare. He suggested that "welfare" carried overtones of waste and inefficiency which "assistance to the poor" did not.

Analyses of media coverage of some important topics have found changes in the prevalence of different frames over time. For example, Gamson and Modigliani (1989) find substantial changes in the way that nuclear power has been discussed in the media. How much these changes have affected the general public is an open question. On the one hand, most people do not pay much attention to political issues, so they may simply not notice changes in media framing. On the other hand, there are cases in which changes in framing provide a plausible explanation of changes in public opinion that would otherwise by difficult to explain. For example, over the last fifty years, opponents of gun control in the United States have used appeals to the Second Amendment to present the issue as one of constitutional rights. During the same time, support for gun control has generally declined, in one of the few examples of a sustained conservative movement in public opinion on an issue. As a result of popular esteem for the Constitution, and especially the Bill of Rights, this way of framing the issue may have been more effective than alternatives such as focusing on the value of guns for self-defense.

The idea of framing suggests that changes in public opinion on particular issues will be accompanied by changes in the patterns of association among opinions: for example, if people increasingly think of gun ownership as a matter of constitutional rights, opposition to gun control should become more closely associated with support for other constitutional rights such as freedom of speech for unpopular groups. Although there has been some scattered discussion of changes in the association among different opinions, there have not been any studies that systematically attempt to investigate the impact of "framing" on this aspect of public opinion. This is an important area for future research.

Summary and Conclusions

The study of change in public opinion is a vibrant research area. The accumulation of a history of repeated survey questions, along with technological advances that have made it easier to identify and analyze relevant data, have opened up new possibilities. Several important conclusions have been established concerning short-term change in opinions, particularly the "thermostatic" reaction and the tendency for opinions in different groups to move in parallel. It has also been possible to establish that there have been trends in public opinion on a number of issues that have continued over fifty years or more, and that the great majority of these trends have been in a liberal direction.

There are also some questions which have not been resolved. One of the most important is the reaction of public opinion to changes in economic conditions, including both general prosperity and recession and the growth of inequality. A second involves the precise meaning of "backlash" and the conditions under which it does or does not take place. A third is whether and how changes in framing by the media or social movements are reflected in public opinion.

5

Long-Term Change in Public Opinion

Chapter 4 considered change in public opinion over the time for which survey data are available. This chapter will consider the possibility that "modernization" – a combination of social changes related to economic growth – affects opinions. This possibility can be assessed by comparing nations or by considering the evidence of history.

Socio-Demographic Change and Public Opinion

Over the long term, socio-demographic change – that is, change in the composition of the population – is a major influence on public opinion. Socio-demographic changes are usually very small from one year to the next but move in the same direction over long periods of time, so that they accumulate to produce a large change. For example, in 1940 only about 25 percent of American adults had a high school diploma and less than five percent had a college degree; today, over 80 percent have a high school diploma and about 35 percent have a college degree. Although there have been changes in terms of many other demographic characteristics including occupation, income, place of residence, and ethnicity, the changes in educational level are particularly important because they have been so large and because education affects a wide range of opinions.

As discussed in previous chapters, early survey research found that more-educated people had more liberal opinions on a number of "social issues," including ethnic and religious tolerance and support for civil liberties, and subsequent research has confirmed these findings. Therefore, the increase in average educational levels helps to explain the liberal trends in opinions on social issues. It does not, however, directly account for all of the changes: if we look at people with the same level of education, some trend usually remains. These trends are generally in the same direction as the educational differences: that is, the opinions of less-educated people move toward the opinions held by educated people, and the opinions of educated people move farther in the same direction. In effect, more-educated people lead the way in terms of opinion. Figure 5.1 illustrates this pattern, showing the percentage who agreed that "a man who admits that he is a homosexual" should be allowed to teach in a college or university among college graduates, high school graduates, and people who did not finish high school between 1973 and 2018. At the beginning of the period, people with more education were more likely to say that a gay

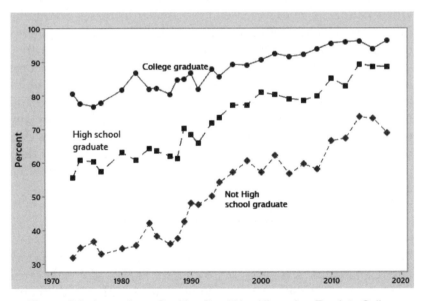

Figure 5.1 Agree that a Gay Man Should be Allowed to Teach in College

Source: compiled with data from the General Social Survey

119

man should be allowed to teach, and as time went on, all educational groups moved in this direction. Thus, one could say that more educated people represented the future.

The fact that the trends within educational groups are usually in the direction of the opinions held by more-educated people suggests that they may indirectly be a result of the rise in educational levels. As the number of college graduates increases, even people who did not attend college will be more likely to have friends or family members who are college graduates, and therefore will be influenced by their opinions. Conversely, college graduates will have fewer friends and family members who did not attend college, and therefore they will be less influenced by their opinions. That is, opinions may be affected, not only by one's own education, but by the average level of education.

Another important demographic change is an increase in average levels of income. For example, median household income in the United States is about 25 percent higher than it was in 1967 (adjusting for inflation), and about twice as high as it was in 1950. Other nations have experienced even greater increases during the same time. Income does not make much difference for opinions on most social issues, but is associated with more conservative opinions on a range of economic issues, so an increase in average income could be expected to produce a conservative trend in opinions on economic issues. This, however, has not occurred: by and large, opinions on economic issues have fluctuated without any trend (see the discussion in Chapter 4). This pattern suggests that opinions on economic issues are influenced by relative rather than absolute income: that is, by how people stand in comparison to the average for their own time.

The Effect of Education on Opinions

Why does education lead to more liberal opinions on social issues? One explanation was proposed by Lipset (1960) and elaborated by Hyman and Wright (1979). It holds that education leads people to develop habits of critical thinking and skills in gathering and assessing information. As a result, more-educated people will be less attached to tradition and more interested in exposing themselves to new information and ideas. This general outlook will make them inclined to have more liberal opinions on many social issues. An alternative view is that the effects of education will differ depending on the content of schooling (Glaeser, Ponzetto, and Shleifer 2007, p. 82). More-educated people will be more likely to accept the prevailing values that are emphasized in school, whatever those values are. In a nation like the United States, the values that are emphasized include equality and civil liberties, but in other cases the prevailing values might involve tradition, respect for authority, or the superiority of a particular ethnic group or religion. In these cases, education would lead to more conservative or even authoritarian opinions.

These different views can be evaluated by comparing the effects of education on opinions in different places or times. Weakliem (2002) examined the effects of education on a range of opinions for about forty nations included in the World Values Survey and found that the tendency for more-educated people to be more liberal on social issues was very widespread. It was stronger in some nations than in others, but was present in all.

Since authoritarian governments generally do not permit surveys, the information about the effects of education is mostly limited to liberal democracies: we do not have information on the effects of education on opinions for cases such as the Soviet Union or apartheid-era South Africa. However, the WVS sample included some nations that had only recently become democracies, including Spain, Portugal, and a number of post-Communist nations. In those nations, older respondents had gone to school when the prevailing values in the educational system did not favor liberalism. If the effects of education represent indoctrination in prevailing values, then more education should have been associated with more authoritarian values among the older generations in these nations. However, there was no evidence that this was the case – people who had gone to school under authoritarian governments were more liberal than their less-educated contemporaries. In conclusion, although it is not possible to say that the effects of education are completely universal, they are quite widespread.

There are several hypotheses about the effects of education on economic opinions. One is that educated people will be more conservative: when comparing two people with the same current income, the one with more education has better earnings prospects and therefore has more reason to oppose redistribution of income (Stinchcombe 1989, p. 170). A second hypothesis is that education promotes general "enlightenment" and empathy, so that it will lead to more liberal views on virtually all issues (Pascarella and Terenzini 1991). A third hypothesis is based on the idea that education and wealth are rival sources of esteem (Hayek 1949). Although education and earnings generally go together, there can be large discrepancies, especially at the highest level: a top student who goes into a professional occupation may earn far less than someone who did not go as far in school and went into business. Educated people will resent these income differences, and consequently favor redistribution, especially when it is directed at reducing the highest incomes. However, they will not support general equality, but a hierarchy based on "merit" rather than success in the marketplace. This view suggests that educated people will be critical of both business and organized labor, and will tend to support government administration and regulation, especially when carried out by "experts."

Research suggests that the effects of education on economic opinions are complex. Weakliem (2002, p. 149) found that more-educated people were more likely to agree that "individuals should take more responsibility for providing for themselves" rather than that "the state should take more responsibility to make sure that everyone is provided for." More-educated people were also more likely to think that it is fair for a more-efficient worker to earn more than a less-efficient colleague. However, education does not lead to conservative opinions on all economic issues: Luttmer (2001) found that more-educated people are more likely to favor increased spending on welfare, compared to less-educated people with the same income.

Contrary to Hayek's hypothesis, it seems that more-educated people have more favorable views of competition and markets, and are less likely to support direct government intervention in the economy. For example, in 2008, a Gallup/USA Today poll asked people if they would be more or less likely to vote for a candidate who supported establishing price controls on gasoline. Among people who did not attend college, 75 percent said they would be more likely to support such a candidate; among people with graduate education, only 43 percent said they would be. Education still affected opinions on this question after controlling for income, and in fact made more difference than income. These differences may reflect greater understanding of how markets work, or may be the result of a more general self-confidence and sense of ability to control one's own life, which are well-established consequences of education (Mirowsky and Ross 1998). Educated people also appear be more inclined to support universal social welfare programs, rather than programs that are limited to specific "deserving" groups (Häusermann and Kriesi 2015). Finally, as discussed in Chapter 2, support for general reduction of income differences seems to be rising among college graduates. Overall, education clearly affects opinions on economic issues, but its effects are not uniformly liberal or conservative.

Finally, education is consistently associated with greater social and political participation (Glaeser, Ponzetto, and Shleifer (2007). Weakliem (2002, p. 153) found that education was associated with lower confidence in some institutions, including the police, organized religion, and the armed forces, but that it made little difference for confidence in parliament or the press. A general interpretation of these differences is that education leads people to value freedom of choice: the institutions in which educated people have less confidence are hierarchical ones that restrict choice.

Modernization and Public Opinion

Although the eighty years covered by surveys is a long time in the life of an individual, it is a short time in terms of human history. The trends that are visible in survey data might be temporary movements when seen from a longer perspective. However, there has been an interrelated group of social changes that have continued for the last several centuries. Major components include advances in science and technology, more rapid communication and transportation, rising material standards of living, and an increase in average levels of education. This group of social changes is often called "modernization." Modernization is a matter of degree – the United States is more "modern" today than it was in 1950, and was more "modern" in 1950 than it had been in 1900. Although some of the individual components may level off in the future – for example, average levels of education cannot increase indefinitely – the general process of modernization can be expected to continue, barring a cataclysmic event such as nuclear war. If modernization affects opinions, then those opinions will show a trend, and those trends can be expected to continue into the future. Modernization has had far-reaching effects on people's lives, so it is reasonable to think that it has also affected opinions in some way. However, some observers argue that any influence it might have will be contingent on a large number of other factors (Blumer 1990). For example, modernization might increase support for democracy under some conditions, and reduce support for democracy under other conditions. Therefore, the question is whether there is any *general* tendency for modernization to be associated with particular opinions.

Comparative Evidence

One way to investigate the relationship between modernization and opinions is to compare nations. Levels of modernization differ widely among nations. The different components of modernization, including educational levels, material affluence, and exposure to the media, tend to be closely associated, so for practical purposes per-capita Gross Domestic Product is usually a good measure of national differences. For example, according to the World Bank, per-capita Gross Domestic Product is about $60,000 in the United States, $18,000 in Mexico, and $6,000 in Nigeria. Given comparable opinion data from different nations, it is possible to see if there is a relationship between modernization and opinions in the contemporary world.

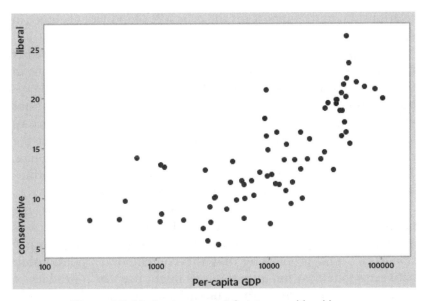

Figure 5.2 Modernization and Opinions on Moral Issues

Source: compiled with data from the World Values Survey, European Values Survey, and World Bank

Research on differences among nations shows a strong and clear association between modernization and support for democracy and civil liberties, gender equality, and tolerance of ethnic and religious minorities (Inglehart 1997). Modernization is also associated with more support for the principle of the individual's right to make choices. Figure 5.2 shows an example. The World Values Survey has questions asking people to rate various actions on a scale running from one ("can never be justified") to ten ("can always be justified"). The sum of the values for four actions that involve individual decisions or consensual agreement – homosexuality, prostitution, divorce, and suicide – can be taken as a measure of commitment to the principle of individual rights to make choices on issues that concern one's own life. The figures on the vertical axis are the mean values of this index in the 73 nations in which the questions were asked. The figures on the horizontal axis are per-capita Gross Domestic Product for that nation. There is a clear relationship: more support for the principle of individual choice in more affluent nations.

If modernization leads to change in opinions, we can predict that, as less developed nations continue to modernize, opinions in those nations will become more like opinions in the more developed nations today. Although it is not possible to be sure about what will happen as the developed nations go beyond their current levels of modernization, there is no definite reason to expect the relationship between modernization and opinions to change. Therefore, it would be reasonable to expect opinions in the affluent nations to continue moving in a liberal direction.

Some observers, however, have raised questions about the possibility of drawing historical conclusions from comparisons of nations, or what Thornton (2001) calls "reading history sideways." The problem is that the contemporary relationship between modernization and opinions might itself be a product of history. Nations such as the United States and Britain acquired prestige by their lead in economic development, which was later enhanced by their success in the Second World War and then in competition with the Soviet Union. Because these nations have been associated with wealth and power, elites and the public in other nations have tried to emulate them – for example, elites send their children to be educated in Britain, France, or the United States, and ordinary people watch and are influenced by American movies and television shows. Therefore, the relationship between modernization and opinions could represent the influence of opinions that prevail in the "leading" nations. This account implies that the cross-national relationship between modernization and opinions might have been different if history had gone differently – for example, if the Soviet Union or Nazi Germany had become the leading world powers. Moreover, it might change in the future if other nations become leaders. For example, if China continues to grow in economic and military strength, then "modernization" might come to be associated with a different set of values.

Historical Evidence

Given this alternative interpretation of contemporary differences among nations, it is necessary to examine the historical record. The process of modernization has been going on in Western Europe for at least the past five hundred years or so. Therefore, if modernization affects opinions, then opinions should have been changing in the same direction over that whole time. Without survey data, it is not possible to measure the precise amount of change, but it is often possible to be reasonably sure about the direction of change. An examination of history suggests that there have been some trends in opinion that have continued for centuries. One involves views of democracy. In 1700, there were no governments that could be called democracies, and there was little popular pressure in favor of democracy. Few observers seem to have even taken it seriously as a possible form of government. By 1900 there were a number of governments that were democracies in the sense of having competitive elections based on a wide franchise; women did not have the right to vote in any of them, and several had significant property requirements for voting, but there was significant popular pressure to remove these limitations. By 2000, there were a large number of democracies, and democracy based on universal suffrage now seems to be regarded as the most legitimate form of government – even authoritarian governments hold elections and sometimes allow limited activity by opposition parties. Monarchy, which was the prevailing form of government for much of human history, has been abolished or reduced to a ceremonial status in all but a few nations.

Another change is growing support for gender equality. In the United States and western Europe, women gained the right to vote, access to education, the ability to enter a wider range of occupations, and equal rights under the law during the nineteenth and twentieth centuries. These are now almost universally accepted as elementary matters of fair treatment: it is hard for people today to imagine how there could ever have been a controversy over women's right to vote. There also seems to have been a long-term increase in ethnic and religious tolerance: for example, in Britain, only members of the Church of England were permitted to serve in Parliament until 1846, when the right was extended to members of other Protestant denominations and to Catholics. In 1858, it was extended to Jews, and in 1888 to atheists and others who were unwilling to "swear by God" in taking their oath of office. As recently as 1960, there was strong and open opposition to the prospect of a Catholic becoming president of the United States (Achen and Bartels 2016, pp. 241–6). Today, it would not be an issue at all.

Another long-term change has been a general growth of "humanitarianism": the belief that it is wrong to impose pain on others (Pinker 2011). For example, in 1700, torture was frequently used in judicial proceedings and slavery was generally accepted. The death penalty was employed against a wide range of offenses, and often carried out by methods designed to make it more painful. In the eighteenth and nineteenth centuries, more voices were raised against these practices. Today, torture and slavery are universally regarded as evil – those who practice them do not defend their actions, but try to keep them hidden. The death penalty has been abolished in most nations – although it continues to be used in the United States, it is employed much less often than in the past, and with an effort to minimize rather than increase suffering.

On economic issues, the range of state responsibility has expanded. Traditionally governments did little to protect people against the hazards of life. Aid to the poor was mostly left to private charity, and there was little government regulation of business. Even the public provision of education was rare until the nineteenth century, and it was controversial at first – some people argued that individuals should be responsible for paying for their own children's education (Cubberley 1922, p. 372). Over the last few centuries, there has been a gradual increase in government regulation of economic activity and protection against poverty, disease, and other kinds of hardship. By the standards that prevailed before the twentieth century, even the conservatives of today support a large and active government.

Modernization and Opinion

To summarize, there is evidence that a number of important changes in general outlook that have continued to move in the same direction over at least the past few hundred years. One aspect of the change can be called individualism: "the individual is generally seen as having a right, or indeed duty, to fulfill himself ... we are no longer identical with our social roles, nor do we automatically accept the rights and duties vested in them" (Crone 1989, pp. 194–5). Another can be called universalism: "the view that all people, and not just one's own kind, are entitled to fair treatment" (Wilson 1993, p. 191). Universalism could also be described as a standard of equal treatment – people should be treated equally unless there is some specific justification for not doing so.

Why would modernization cause a growth of individualism and universalism? One possible factor is that modernization causes changes in the form of social interaction, and that these changes erode traditional status hierarchies. Gellner (1979, p. 32) says that modern society is characterized by "complexity, anonymity, [and] brevity of human encounters," and that in this situation "ranking would be endlessly friction-engendering." The principles of universalism and individualism provide a way for people to get along in the absence of an accepted hierarchy. Moreover, the conditions of modern life also make it easier for people to have privacy and exercise freedom of choice – for example, a factory or office worker living in a city has more freedom than a domestic servant or a peasant living in a small village. Finally, the development of consumer society means that people become used to choosing among goods and services, and are frequently offered new choices. As a result, they are likely to come to think of making choices as an essential part of life and to see any expansion of the range of choice as an opportunity rather than a threat. Kluckhohn (1958, pp. 197), reviewing changes in American values over the twentieth century, saw the rise of "a positive attachment to diversity as a value," and the trend seems to have continued since he wrote.

A second possible factor is that education and advances in communication led people to apply moral intuitions more consistently and more widely (Singer 1981; Pinker 2011). Lerner (1958, p. 50) proposed that a central feature of modernization was "empathy," which he defined as "the capacity to see oneself in the other fellow's situation." The growth of empathy was the result of greater knowledge and more experience in making choices about one's own life. As a result of this broadening of horizons, people found it harder to ignore injustices that occurred outside of their communities, or to believe that other people are fundamentally different from themselves.

General sentiments of individualism and universalism do not automatically lead to particular opinions on specific issues, but in many cases they point strongly in one direction rather than another. For example, ethnic and racial discrimination is hard to reconcile with the principle of universalism. Defenders of discrimination will have to argue that the treatment is "separate but equal," or that certain groups have characteristics that justify unequal treatment, and these kinds of argument can be contested. In contrast, equal treatment needs no special justification: people will accept it as the natural standard of fairness. As a result, support for ethnic discrimination will be more fragile than opposition – people can be persuaded to abandon it, and once they are persuaded, they are unlikely to go back.

The "liberal" trends in opinion that were described earlier in this chapter seem to fit with the principles of individualism and universalism. In particular, the decline in support for ethnic and gender discrimination, growing acceptance of gays and lesbians, and increasing support for civil liberties can be seen as results of one or both principles. Conversely, the opinions that have not shown a trend are ones for which the principles of individualism and universalism provide plausible justifications for either side. For example, opponents of abortion can appeal to the rights of "unborn children," and recently some have suggested that abortion in the case of birth defects amounts to discrimination against the disabled. Jelen and Wilcox (2003, p. 492) note that the rhetoric of abortion opponents has become more secular: "even religious leaders who oppose abortion are increasingly likely to invoke scientific arguments rather than theological ones."

To conclude, there is a strong case that modernization promotes "liberal" opinions on a number of issues. As a result, these liberal trends are likely to continue, and are very unlikely to be reversed. For example, it seems safe to say we will not return to the 1950s in terms of attitudes toward gender. Of course, a trend in opinion on any specific topic cannot continue indefinitely – eventually one position will come to be almost universally accepted. However, the general principle may be taken farther so that new but related issues emerge, as when debate moved from general acceptance of gays and lesbians to same-sex marriage, and then to the rights of transgender people.

Modernization and Economic Opinions

Although the role of the state has expanded enormously in the last few centuries, this change has been affected by factors other than public opinion. First, with the expansion of voting rights, governments felt more pressure to respond to the opinions of the lower classes rather than just the opinions of business and the wealthy. Second, the capacity of the government to regulate business and redistribute income has increased: that is, the government can do more to respond to public demands for action. There may have been some long-term increase in support for government action – questions like the public financing of education or the need for health and safety regulations in the workplace are no longer controversial. However, as discussed in Chapter 4, there has been no clear change in opinions on most economic issues since the middle of the twentieth century. Moreover, in comparisons of nations, the relationship between per-capita GDP and opinions on economic issues is weaker and less consistent than the relationship with opinions on social issues. Overall, the major impact of modernization on opinions involves social rather than economic issues.

Modernization and Nationalism

Many scholars have pointed out that the idea of a "nation" is a modern development (e.g. Znaniecki 1952; Anderson 2006). For most of history, the great majority of people focused on their local communities, and had little sense of being part of a larger nation. The development of national identity was made possible by the growth of education, communication, and geographical mobility.

As national identity developed, some observers thought it was just an intermediate stage in the development of a worldwide community. Lecky (1877[1920], p. 101) saw an expansion of the range of the "benevolent affections" beyond the family to encompass "first a class, then a nation, then a coalition of nations, then all humanity, and finally, its influence is felt in the dealings of man with the animal world." Even today, many people seem to think of nationalism as a relic of the past. However, national identity is a powerful force in the contemporary world, and there is little evidence that it is declining. In fact, Myrdal (1960, pp. 159–77) suggested that the development of the welfare state strengthened national identity: as people give more to other members of their nation and receive more from them, the sense of mutual obligation becomes stronger. Education and the media also continue to be organized by nation: as a result, someone who lives in Boston will be more aware of events in Washington, DC – or even in Texas and California – than in Montreal or Toronto.

"Nationalism" is sometimes understood to involve rivalry and aggression among nations. However, in recent years, the principle that nationalities have the right to self-government has been generally accepted, and aggressive warfare and colonialism are widely condemned. The ideal is that "nations should live together in peace, and, by the active and free exchange of economic and cultural goods, should satisfy each other's needs and develop in the best way their respective talents" (De Ruggiero 1927 [1959], p. 412). That is, nations are seen as partners rather than rivals, but national identity continues to be important.

Immigration and Globalization

In recent decades, international migration levels have increased: some nations are seeing substantial numbers of immigrants for the first time, and others are seeing increased levels of immigration from a wider range of places. Surveys show a widespread feeling that levels of immigration are too high. Citrin and Sides (2008) review data from twenty-five nations and conclude that "the most evident feature . . . is the general desire to decrease immigration." In all twenty-five, the balance of opinion favored a reduction in the number of immigrants. There was no clear pattern in opinions about migration: for example, no consistent difference between more and less affluent nations, or nations with larger or smaller numbers of immigrants.

On the individual level, there are some clear patterns in opinions: people with more education and residents of urban areas are more favorable to immigration. Younger people also tend to be more favorable. These differences suggest that acceptance of immigration will increase as time goes on. In the United States, a number of survey organizations have asked whether immigration should be "kept at its present level, increased or reduced" for more than fifty years. When the question was first asked in 1965, only seven percent said it should be increased, 39 percent said it should be kept at its present level, and 33 percent said it should be decreased. Opinion generally became more negative until the 1990s: in 1994, 63 percent said immigration should be decreased and only six percent said it should be increased. Since that time, support for immigration has steadily grown, despite a rise in the number of immigrants, and in recent years support for an increase has been approximately equal to support for a decrease (Gallup 2019a).

However, looking at a longer range of history casts some doubt on the prediction of a general increase in support for immigration. Many nations adopted stronger restrictions on immigration during the twentieth century. For example, the United States passed restrictive laws in the early 1920s. Because this was before

133

the appearance of surveys, it is not possible to measure the exact level of public support, but the restrictions appear to have been popular (Fetzer 2000, pp. 33–4). This point suggests that levels of support for immigration can rise and fall.

Moreover, the principle that nations have the right to decide on levels of immigration still seems to be widely accepted despite disagreements over what that level should be. Even people who favor higher levels of immigration generally defend their position by pointing to benefits to the nation, or to a national tradition of welcoming immigrants, rather than to a general right to freedom of movement.

Another development of the late twentieth century is "globalization": the development of complex economic relations among nations. This development creates a dilemma for national governments – they have to satisfy their voters while working within constraints imposed by international relations. This issue is particularly prominent in members of the European Union, but is relevant in almost all nations. Although there is less evidence on this issue than on immigration, it seems that public opinion is ambivalent, combining general support for international organizations with a desire to maintain national autonomy.

Summary and Conclusions

Education is an important influence on long-term change in opinions. Education is associated with more liberal opinions on a number of "social issues." Although these effects are not completely universal, they seem to hold widely. Education also affects opinions on economic issues: more-educated people generally have more positive views of markets, but are now not much different in terms of opinions about the redistribution of income. Since educational levels are almost certain to increase, these effects will influence the future course of public opinion.

Long-term changes in public opinion are difficult to study systematically, partly because of limitations of data – there are only a few nations with a substantial history of opinion surveys – and partly because many changes are gradual, so that they cannot be linked to specific events. However, there is strong evidence that "modernization" – a complex of changes associated with economic development – is associated with changes in public opinion, most of them involving movement in what would usually be called a liberal direction. I have proposed that these changes can be understood as a growth of "individualism" and "universalism," but this characterization needs to be refined and tested. To some extent, this may be done by comparing public opinion in different nations but, given the potential problems with "reading history sideways," it is also necessary to use historical data to make inferences about changes in public opinion, as attempted by Kluckhohn (1958), and more recently by Pinker (2011) and Fischer (2010).

6

Public Opinion and Liberal Democracy

Over the past two centuries, there has been a movement toward democracy. Democratic governments have become more common and have shown the power to endure: a nation that has experienced several decades of democracy is very likely to remain a democracy. The movement toward democracy has not been steady, and there have been some intervals in which it seems to have stalled or even reversed, but the general trend is clear. Nevertheless, in recent years there have been definite signs of strain even in long-established and previously successful democracies. This chapter will discuss the causes of strain and their implications for the future of democratic government.

Changes in Europe

Mair (2013, pp. 17–44), in a review of political developments in Europe, sees a trend toward "citizen disengagement," in which people withdraw from politics. In many democracies, there have been declines in voter participation, satisfaction with government performance, and general trust in government (Pharr and Putnam 2000). Traditional political parties have lost support – for example, in Germany the Social Democratic Party and Christian Democratic Party had a combined total of more than 80 percent of the votes during the 1970s and 1980s, but fell to barely over 50 percent by 2017. The decline of traditional parties has been accompanied by a rise of new parties, but most of these have not been able to maintain a stable base of support. As a result, there has been an increase in electoral volatility, with large swings in overall party support from one election to the next. For example, in 2012, the French Socialist party won almost half of the seats in the National Assembly, its best performance in thirty years; in 2017, it won only about five percent of the seats, its worst performance ever. There has also been a decline in voter turnout: in Germany, it has fallen from about 90 percent in the 1970s to about 70 percent in recent elections.

An optimistic interpretation of this situation is that voters have changed, but that the major parties have not kept up with them (Dalton 2014). Since the 1960s, new ideas and issues have emerged, including environmentalism, gender equality, and gay and lesbian rights. Although the major parties have paid some attention to these new issues, their primary focus continues to be the traditional economic issues: redistribution of income and the regulation of business. As a result, there is a mismatch between the concerns of ordinary citizens and the concerns of the parties, so voters have become discontented and are searching for alternatives. When the political system provides a better fit to public opinion, either because of the emergence of new parties or adaption by old parties, a new balance will be restored.

There are, however, several facts that are hard to reconcile with this interpretation. First, many of the most successful new parties, such as the National Rally in France (formerly the National Front), appeal to ethnic or religious prejudice. In some cases, the leaders of these parties have had ties to neo-Nazi or other extremist movements. Second, when new parties have gained office, they have usually failed to provide effective or stable government. For example, Silvio Berlusconi, a businessman with no previous political experience, founded a new political party and became Prime Minister of Italy in 1994. Berlusconi was successful as a politician, serving for a total of nine years between 1994 and 2011, but his government was generally regarded as corrupt and ineffective (Stille 2006). He was eventually forced from office and convicted on corruption charges. Third, even when traditional parties have attempted to respond to popular demands, whether by changing their ideological position or by allowing more public participation in the selection of leaders, they have still been unable to regain the loyalty of voters. For example, during the late twentieth and early twenty-first centuries the British Labour Party won elections by moving to the center, but in the 2010 and 2015 elections it lost by large margins despite continuing its centrist orientation. In response, it selected a new leader using a process that allowed more popular participation than ever before. This process resulted in the victory of a left-winger who was unpopular among party insiders. Under the new leadership, Labour did much better in the 2017 elections, but very poorly in 2019. That is, there does not seem to be any clear formula for the parties to reconnect with public opinion: whatever they do, the long-term decline continues.

Taken together, these points suggest that popular "disengagement" may be an enduring feature of modern societies. Mair (2013, p. 141) speaks of "a growing divide . . . between parties which claim to represent, but don't deliver, and those which deliver, but are no longer seem to represent."

Changes in the United States

In many ways the United States has followed a distinctive course. In the 1990s, there were signs that the traditional parties were declining. In 1992, Ross Perot, an independent candidate with no previous political experience, received 19 percent of the vote for President. His support fell to eight percent of the vote when he ran again in 1996, but by historical standards that was still a strong showing for an independent candidate. Independent candidates also had some success at the state level: one was elected Governor of Maine in 1994 and re-elected in 1998, and another was elected Governor of Minnesota in 1998. Bernie Sanders, an independent who identified as a socialist, was elected to the House of Representatives from Vermont in 1988.

However, in the twenty-first century, the two major parties have restored and even strengthened their position. After Ross Perot, no third-party candidate for president has received more than about three percent of the vote. In 2016, some conservatives were alarmed by the nomination of Donald Trump as the Republican candidate for president and tried to recruit a prominent figure to run as an independent, but they were unsuccessful. Traditionally, many Americans "split" their votes, picking candidates of different parties for different offices, but this practice has become less common. People have also become less likely to switch parties from one election to the next: since 2000, all presidential elections have been close, with no major party candidate receiving less than 46 percent or more than 53 percent of the vote. Voter turnout has remained steady or increased since the 1970s, although it is still low by international standards. Thus, in the past twenty years, Americans seem to have become more, rather than less, firmly attached to the two major parties.

However, the growing strength of American parties seems to involve fear or distrust of the other party rather than positive support for one's own party. As discussed in Chapter 3, the percentage of people who give the parties the lowest possible rating on a "feeling thermometer" has increased sharply in the twenty-first century (see Figure 3.2). People also have more negative opinions about individual candidates. Since 1956, the Gallup Poll has asked people to rate the presidential candidates of each party on a scale of -5 to +5; the number giving the highest possible ratings had declined, while the number giving the lowest possible ratings has increased. In 2012, although Barack Obama had more positive than negative ratings, he had almost as many -5 ratings as Barry Goldwater had in 1964. In 2016, many observers thought that Donald Trump's supporters were unusually enthusiastic; however, only 11 percent gave him a +5, the lowest figure of any candidate except for Goldwater (Weakliem 2010–2019, December 25, 2018).

One trend has been similar in the United States and Europe: the decline in general confidence in government. The American National Election Studies include a number of questions about general confidence in government going back to the 1950s – for example: "How much of the time do you think you can trust the

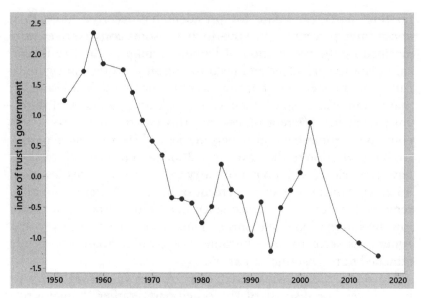

Figure 6.1 Confidence in Government, 1952–2016

Source: compiled with data from American National Election Studies

government in Washington to do what is right?", "Would you say that the government is pretty much run by a few big interests looking out for themselves or that it is run for the benefit of all the people?", and "People like me don't have any say about what the government does." A combined index of confidence based on these questions is shown in Figure 6.1. Confidence fell in the 1960s and 1970s, and reached a low in 1994. It then increased in the late 1990s and early 2000s, but declined again and reached a new low in 2016.

The Results of Popular Discontent

To summarize, popular discontent with government has increased in both Europe and the United States, but it has been expressed in different ways: in Europe by the decline of traditional parties and in the United States by insurgent movements within the parties.

These different expressions may reflect differences in political institutions. In the United States, it is difficult for third parties to gain representation in Congress because of the use of single-member districts. At the same time, candidates for most offices are chosen by primary elections rather than selected by party leaders. As a result, the most promising path for an "outsider" is to gain the nomination of one of the major parties rather than to found a new party. Successful challenges have become more common in recent years, especially among Republicans. In 2010, candidates affiliated with a new conservative movement known as the "Tea Party" won the Republican nomination for a substantial number of seats in the House of Representatives and Senate, in some cases defeating Republican incumbents; in 2016 Donald Trump won the Republican nomination for President despite initial opposition from almost all party leaders and elected officials.

Populism

The new political parties and movements that have appeared in recent years are often called "populist." Most of these have been on the right, including the National Rally in France, the Alternative for Germany, and the Danish People's Party. However, the term has also been applied to some left-wing parties, such as Syriza in Greece, and to some that are difficult to classify in ideological terms, such as the Five Star Movement in Italy.

The term "populism" was first applied in the late 1800s as a nickname for the People's Party in the United States. The original populists advocated for the interests of farmers and favored the regulation of large corporations, and initially most historical counts regarded them favorably (Woodward 1959). However, a more critical view of populism became prominent in the 1950s, and today "populism" is usually a negative term. This history of usage raises the question of whether "populism" has any central meaning or is just an epithet. Many different definitions of populism have been proposed, but a common theme is that populist movements see a conflict between "the people" and a small elite which is regarded as corrupt, untrustworthy, and possibly unpatriotic. Oliver and Rahn (2016, p. 190) provide a good summary: "at its core, populism is a type of political rhetoric that pits a virtuous 'people' against nefarious, parasitic elites who seek to undermine the rightful sovereignty of the common folk."

To some extent, almost all contenders for contenders for office in democracies use "populist" rhetoric. However, there are clearly differences of degree: mainstream candidates promise to "stand up to special interests," but do not suggest that those interests are fundamentally illegitimate. Populists, in contrast, treat the "elite" as something that should be destroyed rather than restrained.

Political Sources of Populism

One source of populism is a discrepancy between the views held by political elites and those held by the public. As Douthat (2017) puts it "some set of ideas commands public support but lacks purchase in elite policy debates. Then a combination of elite failure and popular pressure makes that tension ripe for exploitation, and some new figure or movement emerges, promising to follow the will of the people and override the ruling class." In this perspective, populism is not fundamentally different from mainstream political movements: like them, it involves the pursuit of policy goals. However, since those goals have few advocates among political elites, populist movement will usually have to rely on inexperienced leaders. Supporters of populist movements are also likely to have feelings of animosity and resentment toward the elites who have been ignoring or resisting their demands. As a result, populist movements may have some tendency to attract extremist or irrational elements, but these are not essential features.

This view suggests that populist movements may make a positive contribution to politics by being a source of new ideas and new leadership. For example, the American populists of the late nineteenth century called for government action to help people affected by economic downturns. This demand went against the economic orthodoxy of the time, but had a strong appeal to the public, and has since come to be widely accepted by political elites.

From a contemporary perspective, the economic policies proposed by the populists seem more reasonable than the "mainstream" policies of the time. Of course, this does not mean that all populist movements will make a positive contribution: that depends on the specific nature of their ideas. However, this analysis implies that populism can be absorbed into the political system if political elites make compromises and adopt some populist proposals.

Social Sources of Populism

Another possible source of support for populism is a decline, or threat of decline, in social standing : "Groups that are dispossessed invariably seek targets on whom they can vent their resentments, targets whose power can serve to explain their dispossession" (Bell 1964, p. 3). These targets are generally not the real source of their problems, which may be the result of broad social changes rather than the actions of any specific group. Bell (1964, p. 16) said that "what the right wing is fighting . . . is essentially 'modernity' . . . and what it seeks to defend is its fading dominance, exercised once through the institutions of small-town America, over the control of social change."

Many accounts of support for contemporary right-wing populism offer a similar analysis. For example, Mutz (2018, p. 1) explained support for Donald Trump by "issues related to American global dominance and the rise of a majority–minority America: issues that threaten white Americans' sense of dominant group status." Maintaining dominant ethnic or national status was particularly important to voters who did not have alternative sources of status: that is, to less-educated and blue-collar whites (Mutz 2018, p. 9).

A similar analysis can be applied to left-wing populism. Disadvantaged groups such as the poor or ethnic minorities can also "seek targets" to blame for their condition. From this perspective, the key feature of populism is that it is punitive – it focuses on assigning blame and inflicting punishment rather than finding solutions to problems. Conventional politics of both the left and the right involves the more or less rational pursuit of goals and interests, while populism is an expression of anger or frustration.

Lipset and Raab (1970) provided a concise summary of this analysis in the title of their book on right-wing movements in the United States: *The Politics of Unreason*. The idea of populism as punitive suggests that populist movements can combine elements of left and right or quickly shift between those poles, since they appeal to emotions that can be directed at various targets. Lipset (1970, pp. 380–1) noted that the nineteenth-century populists frequently appealed to anti-Semitism, and that some of their leaders eventually became racists or nativists, and some observers see a growth of anti-Semitism among contemporary left-wing populist movements.

Social Capital and Support for Populism

This analysis suggests that potential support for populism will be related to the strength of community, or what is sometimes called "social capital" (Putnam 2000). When there is an active community life involving local politics, voluntary organizations, or simply informal interaction, people will have more sense of understanding and efficacy: they will respond to problems by conventional political activity. Where community life is weak, people will feel that their lives are controlled by remote and mysterious forces, and therefore will be more likely to turn to populist movements. Moreover, community life provides people with a sense of purpose and belonging; if it declines, they may turn to politics as a substitute. Many accounts of contemporary politics in the United States suggest rising polarization and distrust are the result of a decline in community. For example, the publicity material for a book by Senator Ben Sasse (2018) says: "Contrary to conventional wisdom, our crisis is not really about politics . . . we're so lonely we can't see straight – and it bubbles out as anger . . . As traditional tribes of place evaporate, we rally against common enemies so we can feel part of a team."

Has there actually been a decline of community? Putnam (2000) found evidence that membership in some kinds of organizations has declined in the United States since the middle of the twentieth century. Some observers, however, argue that there has been an increase in other kinds of organizations, and in some kinds of informal social interaction (Fischer 2011). In any case, individuals who have fewer social ties do not seem to be more likely to support populist movements: they are simply less involved in politics (Rydgren 2009).

Ties among people can differ in quality as well as in number, but measuring, or even defining, the quality of community is difficult. Many people believe that communities are not as close as they once were, but this could merely be nostalgia: similar concerns have been voiced for centuries. Probably the best evidence of potential changes in the quality of community is provided by a question that has regularly been included in the General Social Survey: "Would you say that most people can be trusted or that you can't be too careful in dealing with people?" The share saying that "most people can be trusted" has declined from about 45 percent in the early 1970s to just over 30 percent today, and somewhat different forms of the questions which were asked before the GSS began suggest that trust has been declining since the 1950s (Fischer 2010). When comparing places – nations or regions within nations – higher average levels of trust are associated with successful democracy, as well as many other measures of the quality of life (Putnam 2000). However, while it is reasonable to think that the decline of general trust in people has had some negative impact on American politics, it is not clear whether it helps to explain populism. On the individual level, trust does not have a strong connection to political views: in the 2016 presidential election, there was almost no difference between supporters of Hillary Clinton and Donald Trump in average levels of trust.

Even if there is little or no relationship between trust and support for populism at the individual level, it is possible that there is a relationship at the level of places. That is, places in which the average level of trust is lower may have a lower quality of community life, and people may respond to the low quality of community life by giving more support to populist parties. There is some evidence that this is the case. Berning and Ziller (2017) find that higher neighborhood social trust is associated with lower support for right-wing populist parties in the Netherlands. Although they do not have a direct measure of trust, Durante, Pinotti, and Tesei

(2019) find that places which got earlier access to the television network owned by Silvio Berlusconi later gave greater support, not only to Berlusconi's own party, but also to a subsequent populist party, the Five Star Movement. They suggest that exposure to the network, which focused on low-quality entertainment, led to more general changes in outlook, such as a weaker sense of community, more cynicism about politics, or a taste for simplistic rhetoric.

Historical Factors and Support for Populism

Most of the social changes that have been suggested as sources of populism are gradual: for example, the ethnic diversity of the American population has been increasing for at least the last fifty years, and "modernity" has been advancing for centuries. Therefore, in order to explain why populist movements appear or decline at particular times, it is necessary to consider some factors that can change quickly. One potentially important factor is confidence in political elites: people will turn to populist movements when they do not trust the traditional leaders. Figure 6.1 shows that confidence in government can rise or fall quickly, although there has been a long-term tendency to decline since the 1950s. A second factor is historical events which focus attention on particular concerns: for example, the increase in the number of refugees in recent years has made immigration a more important issue in a number of European nations. Another potentially important event was the election of Barack Obama: some observers hold that having a black president made whites more conscious of the prospect of losing their dominant status (Wetts and Willer 2018).

The Response to Populism

The idea that populism is a response to social decline suggests that populist movements are largely destructive. If they gain office, they are likely to be unsuccessful, since their policies do not address the real problems of their supporters. In order to retain power, they will have to keep mobilizing their supporters against new targets. This analysis also suggests that mainstream parties cannot win back support from populist movements by compromising with them or adopting some of their positions, since populist movements are not primarily about specific positions, but a reflection of general discontent that can easily be turned against other targets. The only way to reduce support for populist movements is to change the underlying social conditions that created them.

The distinction between political and social sources of populism is relevant to contemporary debates about the responses to populist movement. In Europe, the question is whether mainstream parties should try to accommodate populist parties by adopting some of their positions or including them as partners in government, or should combine to keep them out of power. In the United States, it is whether the Democratic party should try to win back the voters who turned to Donald Trump in 2016 (mostly less-educated whites in rural areas and small towns), or should write them off and focus on mobilizing a coalition of ethnic minorities and the educated middle class.

Public Opinion and Elite Opinion

The idea that populism results from a gap between the opinions of the public and political elites raises the question of why there would be a difference between popular and elite opinions. In a democracy, there are two forces that work to reduce the gap between public and elite opinion. The first is that candidates for office have an incentive to offer the public what it wants. The second is that, on many issues, political leaders can persuade their followers.

Nevertheless, there are some issues on which there is an elite consensus that differs from average public opinion. Stouffer (1955) found that support for the civil liberties of people accused of Communist sympathies was greater among both Republican and Democratic elites than among the general public. More recently, support for free trade has been much higher among political elites than among the public (Weakliem 2010–2019, May 3, 2019). Differences between elite opinion and public opinion may reflect the principles of elites. This is presumably the major explanation of differences over civil liberties: elites had a deeper understanding of specific constitutional protections and the general importance of civil liberties. In other cases, the differences may reflect the influence of expert opinion or the lessons of experience in government. These factors help to explain the differences on trade: economists are almost universally opposed to tariffs, and politicians of both parties may be concerned that raising tariffs would lead to problems in relations with our allies.

Elite Opinion in Europe

In many European nations, a strong consensus seems to have developed among political elites on several issues. One is support for the European Union and the goal of an "ever-closer union." This consensus also seems to extend to other elite groups, including high-ranking civil servants, leading academics, and journalists and editors. The public, however, is more divided: there are some strong opponents of European integration, and many others with mixed opinions. Alesina and Wacziarg (2000, p. 167) observed that "there is mounting evidence that the average European voter is and has for some time been much less enthusiastic about European integration and monetary union than his or her leaders." Since they wrote, the gap between public and elite opinion on the issue has probably increased rather than declined. Anderson and Hecht (2018) compile a general index of public opinion on European integration, and find that it has become slightly less favorable since the 1970s in France, Germany, and Italy, and has fluctuated without any clear trend in Britain. Guiso, Sapienza, and Zingales (2016) find that evaluations of the EU generally became less favorable after the 1992 Maastricht treaty, and have never recovered. At the same time, elite opinion seems to have become steadily more committed to integration. For example, Hyman (2010, pp. 20) says that trade union leaders have shifted from "suspicion or even antagonism towards acceptance and even enthusiasm."

Another issue on which there is a substantial gap between European political elites and the public is immigration. As Citrin and Sides (2008, p. 51) observe, "there is a disjunction between public opinion and the dominant view of political elites, which tend to be much more favorable to immigrants." A third is general economic policy. There seems to be an economic consensus among political elites in favor of what is sometimes called "neoliberalism": restraining budget deficits, reducing the regulation of labor markets, and slowing or reversing the growth of the welfare state. After the recession of 2008–2009, most European governments followed a policy of "austerity" rather than trying to stimulate the economy. People who disagree with the elite consensus on any or all of these issues have turned to populist parties to express their views.

Elite Opinion in the United States

In the United States, consensus among political elites seems to have declined in recent decades. For example, for many years surveys have found that most people thought that the government was not doing enough to stop illegal immigration. In response, Republican officeholders took a harder line on immigration: in 2013 Republicans in the House of Representatives refused to consider a bill that created a "path to citizenship" that had been passed by a bipartisan majority in the Senate. Although Donald Trump gave more emphasis to the issue than other candidates in the 2016 election, by that time his general "get tough" orientation was not unusual among Republicans. Thus, the sentiments that have contributed to the growth of populist parties in other nations have been absorbed by the party system in the United States.

Traditionally, ideological divisions between parties were smaller in the United States than in Europe: both American parties were loose coalitions with no official doctrine. Moreover, the overall range of ideological positions was smaller: even the most liberal Democratic politicians disavowed the "socialist" label and did not advocate positions such as public ownership of industry or national economic planning. However, ideological differences between the mainstream parties have declined in Europe, mostly because the parties of the left have moved to the center, dropping commitments to socialism and weakening ties with trade unions. This is a continuation of a long process. When socialist parties arose in the late nineteenth and early twentieth centuries, they sought a fundamental transformation to public ownership and control of economic activity. As time went on, they came to accept a primary role for markets and private ownership, and parties of the right accepted higher levels of redistribution and government regulation of business. In the United States, the pattern is very different: since the middle of the twentieth century, the parties have moved farther apart on many issues, and the divergence seems to be continuing. Many accounts of American politics have noted the ideological divergence of the parties, but there have been few attempts to explain why the United States is different from other nations in this respect.

Explaining Ideological Divergence in the United States

There are several factors that limit ideological divergence between parties. One is the experience of government. Parties will discover that some of their promises were unrealistic, or at least difficult to achieve, and will therefore try to persuade their supporters to accept more limited reforms. Another is the need to compete for votes: parties will try to appeal to the "swing voters" in the middle, who make the difference between victory and defeat (Downs 1957).

Emergence of New Issues

Less attention has been paid to the forces that might cause ideological divergence among parties, but the literature on public opinion suggests two possible answers. One builds on the idea of a "life history of issues" proposed by Berelson, Lazarsfeld, and McPhee (1954, pp. 207–12; see also Zaller 1992 and Zaller 2012).

Putting a new issue on the political agenda requires the support of a committed minority, and committed minorities often take extreme positions. Therefore, as a new issue appears, ideological divergence will tend to grow, as one party takes up the issue and the other opposes it. However, as the issue becomes a standard part of politics, partisan polarization will decline. One reason is that if popular support for the new idea continues to grow, the party that opposes it will de-emphasize the issue or moderate its position. Another is that compromises can be proposed and implemented, reducing the pressure for change.

This account suggests that the appearance of new issues leads to partisan divergence. When many new issues appear, the parties will diverge; when there are few new issues, the parties will converge. The social changes of the 1960s and 1970s put many issues on the agenda, and since then new ones have continued to appear, partly because of what Fine (2006) speaks of as the "chaining of social problem," in which the apparent resolution of one controversial issue gives rise to other issues. For example, as acceptance of gay and lesbian people increased, same-sex marriage became an issue; as the principle of same-sex marriage came to be accepted, discrimination against same-sex couples by private business became an issue. A distinctive feature of the United States is that the leaders of political parties have less control over the political agenda: issues can be brought to attention by social movements, individual politicians, or the courts. For example, the issue of same-sex marriage first became visible as a result of state court cases. Moreover, when a policy is enacted, opponents have many ways in which they can resist. For example, after health-care reform was passed in 2010, opponents continued to fight in state governments and in the courts.

Thus, partisan divergence in the United States may have occurred because more new issues became and remained the subject of public controversy. If the issues came up in other nations, they were more likely to be dealt with by political elites with less public debate, and opponents of the elite consensus had less power to keep them alive by continued resistance.

Growth in the Importance of Social Issues

A second possible explanation for ideological divergence in the United States is a growth in the relative importance of "social issues." Some observers argue that such issues produce more intense polarization than economic issues, because they involve moral values. Lipset (1970, pp. 231–2) said "to work out compromises over wages and hours or tax policy is easy. To compromise with what is held to be heresy or a basic threat to the right way of life is much more difficult." Zakaria (2017) recently offered a very similar analysis: "When the core divide was economic, you could split the difference. If one side wanted to spend $100 billion and the other wanted to spend zero, there was a number in between . . . But if the core issues are about identity, culture and religion (think of abortion, gay rights, Confederate monuments, immigration, official languages), then compromise seems immoral." Although "social issues" have become more prominent in Europe as well, they may have a larger role in the United States because of the importance of religion in American life. This analysis suggests that ideological divergence in the United States was a result of a reaction of the "religious right" against the social changes of the 1960s and 1970s.

There are, however, several features of recent American history that do not fit either of these explanations. One is that there has been no sign of convergence on many long-standing social issues: for example, the parties are farther apart on abortion now than they were in the 1970s, and the change of a bipartisan compromise seems more remote. A second is that partisan polarization has increased on many economic issues as well as on social issues.

For example, Medicare (the government health-care program for people over 65) was controversial when it was proposed in the 1960s. However, after it became law, the controversy soon faded: conservatives made no effort to repeal the program or scale it back, and the scope of benefits was substantially expanded under the Republican administration of Richard Nixon. In contrast, after the Affordable Care Act ("Obamacare") was passed in 2010,

Republicans made numerous attempts to stop it, including direct votes to repeal it, efforts to cut off funding, and court cases alleging that the act was unconstitutional. A decade after its passage, the controversy continues, and the Republican Party is still committed to repeal of the Affordable Care Act. This program was essentially an economic policy, and one involving many complex technical details: exactly the kind of issue on which it seems like it should have been possible to "split the difference." Another economic policy that was the subject of intense controversy was the Obama administration's attempt to stimulate the economy by increased public spending; it was not only opposed by almost all Republicans in Congress, but also provided the spark that created the "Tea Party" movement.

As these examples suggest, both economic and political issues can be more or less "moralized." Economic issues can be seen in light of moral questions such as whether the beneficiaries of a government program are deserving, whether the tax burden is fair, and whether government regulations infringe on property rights. Conversely, social issues do not have to be seen in terms of morality. For example, in the 1970s and 1980s, the reaction to increased drug use was a "war on drugs" with harsh penalties for sellers and users; more recently, the increase in opioid addiction has generally been treated as a public health issue.

Constitutional Originalism

Several recent observers have argued that a conservative ideology, in the sense of a set of principles that can be applied to concrete political issues, has developed in the United States. Traditionally, the left has been more concerned with general principles: conservatism has been just a general inclination to favor the status quo and be skeptical of proposals for change. In recent decades, however, there seems to have been a change in conservative thinking. Since the 1980s, conservative legal thinkers have developed a position of "originalism," which holds that the Constitution places definite limits on the power of the government, especially the Federal government. In this view "legislation contravening the Constitution as originally understood by the Founders [is] ripe for aggressive voiding on the grounds of fidelity," even if it is of long standing and has been upheld in previous court decisions (Kersch 2014, p. 1098). Although most discussions of originalism have focused on legal thought, it may also have influenced popular thinking. As Kristol (1995, p. 376) observes, "the United States is a 'creedal' nation": that is, national identity is understood as a matter of ideals rather than just birth or ancestry. The Constitution has a special place in that creed: people often speak of it in quasi-religious terms (Ellis 2018). The creedal outlook creates a possibility of "fundamentalist" movements which hold that it is necessary to go back to the canonical texts in order to find the answers to contemporary problems. Moreover, originalists have developed a broader historical account in which a turn away from the "correct" interpretation of the Constitution in the early twentieth century led to profound negative changes in American society (Kersch 2014, pp. 1101–03). Thus, the defense of the constitution can be connected to a more general ideological outlook.

The Two-Party System

Another possibility is that the ideological divergence results from the strength of the two-party system in the United States. Downs (1957) argued that a two-party system produces ideological convergence, since both parties have an incentive to appeal to voters in the middle. Another way to compete, however, is to convince voters that the opposing party is unacceptable. Wilson (1995, p. x) suggests that "the motive force of any incentive, but especially ideology, is greater when people perceive a threat to remove what they have than when they hear a promise to bestow what they want." If this is the case, then presenting the other party as a threat may be a more attractive strategy than moving to the center. In principle, a party might try to do both: to move to the center while saying that the other party was extreme. However, in order to make charges of extremism effective, a party will have to create some ideological distance from the other party: for example, by taking steps to defend and strengthen a program that is allegedly under attack.

The United States is unusual in terms of the strength of the two leading parties. In nations with a parliamentary system, smaller parties have a chance of gaining representation and potentially holding the balance of power, and in nations with multiple rounds of presidential voting, such as France, they can influence the outcome of the first round. In these cases, attacking another party is a less effective way to gain strategy: even if attacks are effective, the votes may go to other parties. In fact, since voters often dislike negative campaigning, a party that attacks too vigorously may lose some of its own supporters. In the United States, however, a vote for a third party is almost always a "wasted vote": someone who is determined to keep one major-party candidate out of office has no alternative but to vote for the other major-party candidate.

Consequently, a two-party system may have a tendency for ideological divergence rather than convergence. This hypothesis raises a question of why the American parties did not start to diverge until recently. A possible answer is that for most of American history, many people voted on the basis of local concerns or ethnic, religious, or regional loyalties. The potential for divergence did not take effect until large numbers of people started to focus on national politics and to think in ideological terms.

Democratic Government in Modern Society

Ironically, the ideological convergence of European parties and the divergence of American parties have both produced popular dissatisfaction. In Europe, dissatisfaction arises because choices among the parties do not seem to make a difference; in the United States, because party differences lead to conflict and "gridlock." A decline of confidence in democratic governments has occurred in many nations, and despite ups and downs in the short term, there is a definite downward trend. The widespread decline in confidence in government raises a question about the future of democracy.

Growing Support for Authoritarianism?

Some observers suggest that frustration with the perceived failures of democratic governments will lead people to turn toward non-democratic alternatives. Foa and Mounk (2017, p. 5) see signs of "growing popular disaffection with liberal-democratic norms and institutions, and of increasing support for authoritarian interpretations of democracy." These interpretations appeal to the principle of popular rule, but hold that the "will of the people" is embodied in a single leader, so that opposition to that leader is opposition to the people.

There are several nations, including Hungary, Russia, and Turkey, in which democratically elected leaders have been able to consolidate power by making it harder for opposition parties to compete in elections, restricting the freedom of the press, and attacking on the independence of the courts. However, none of the nations in which this process has occurred has had a long history of democracy. In Italy, Silvio Berlusconi seemed to have authoritarian inclinations, but he always met strong opposition, and eventually lost his parliamentary majority and resigned. In the United States, Donald Trump has made threats against newspapers and television networks, the courts, and political opponents, but has rarely acted on them. The intention behind the threats might have been to rally popular support by attacks on "elites" but, if so, he has been unsuccessful: his approval ratings have remained below 50 percent during his entire time in office.

Although the Italian and American experiences suggest that there are strong barriers to the development of authoritarianism, they also indicate that there is significant popular dissatisfaction with conventional political leaders. Does this mean that there is a more general decline in support for democracy? The World Values Survey has asked people to rate different kinds of government on a scale running from one ("very bad") to four ("very good"). Figure 6.2 shows the average rating of democracy as a form of government in eight affluent democracies. In seven of them, there has

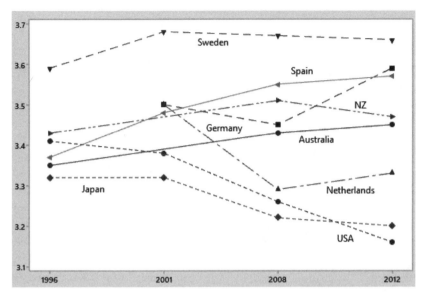

Figure 6.2 Ratings of Democracy as a Form of Government

Source: compiled with data from World Values Survey

been no change or a small increase, but the United States shows a large and consistent decline, and now gives the least favorable ratings to democracy as a form of government. However, ratings of democracy as a form of government are still strongly favorable, even in the United States: in all nations, the average is above three ("good").

The WVS also asks respondents to rate "having the army rule" as a form of government, and the national averages are shown in Figure 6.3. Again, there is a difference in the trends in the United States and other nations. Only the United States shows a clear trend, and it is an increase: compared to other nations it was about average in the 1990s but is now most favorable to military rule. The average rating of military rule is still lower than the rating for democracy, but the gap is substantially smaller than it was in the 1990s. This comparison raises a question of why the United States is distinctive. One possibility is that partisan conflict leads to an increase in support for non-partisan institutions. The American

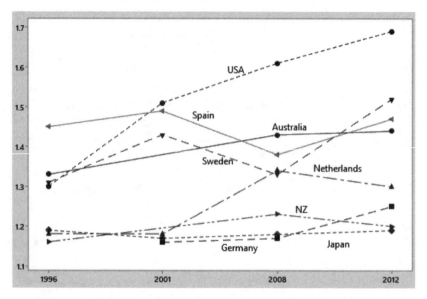

Figure 6.3 Ratings of Rule by the Army as a Form of Government

Source: compiled with data from World Values Survey

military has a strong tradition of staying out of politics, so its prestige has risen as political polarization has increased.

Growing Demand for Participatory Democracy?

Other observers hold that popular discontent does not involve the principle of democracy, but specific forms of representative democracy. People want governments to be more responsive to their wishes, so new institutions will have to be developed that give ordinary people a larger voice in government (Dalton 2014). When he ran for President in 1992, Ross Perot proposed "electronic town meetings," in which people could listen to experts, debate among themselves, and vote on policy proposals. This would have been difficult with the technology of the time, but the development of the internet has made it a realistic possibility.

However, although most people favor more popular participation in principle, they are reluctant actually to engage in it.

Political discussion necessarily involves disagreement, and it is rarely possible to find a solution that leaves everyone satisfied, or even moderately satisfied. In everyday life, most people try to avoid discussing politics, or restrict their discussions to people who agree with them (Eliasoph 1998). Although the idea of participatory democracy has attracted the interest of political theorists, it does not seem to have much appeal to the general public. Hibbing and Theiss-Morse (2002) describe the popular ideal as "stealth democracy": leaders do what the people want without requiring the public to participate.

Continued Growth of Representative Democracy?

Another possibility is the continuation and further spread of electoral democracy. Experience has shown that even a democracy in which most people are not particularly active or well informed can produce effective and reasonably responsive government. One factor that makes this possible is an effective party system, in which parties respond to general sentiments from the public – for example, "help the poor" or "control immigration" – and translate them into workable policies. Although it is difficult to measure effectiveness, it seems that many democracies have lost ground in this respect. As a result of globalization, national governments are simultaneously facing more complex problems and operating under more constraints, and have often fallen short in terms of either responsiveness or ability to develop and implement policies. Nevertheless, despite globalization, national governments still have a good deal of freedom to develop their own policies (Rodrik 2011). Moreover, the development of international organizations allows more effective action to meet global problems: responses to the recession of 2008–2009, despite their shortcomings, were far more effective than responses to the Great Depression had been (Drezner 2014). Partly as a result, the authoritarian movements of today have been less widespread and less successful than the authoritarian movements of the 1920s and 1930s.

Although the contemporary problems with democratic

governments are serious ones, there is an underlying reason for optimism. The climate of public opinion is not the only factor that affects the prospects for democracy, but it is an important one, and it is more favorable today than it was in the past. Changes in public opinion show a clear trend in the direction of increasing "enlightenment": less ethnic and religious prejudice, more tolerance of unpopular opinions, and more acceptance of the general principle of equal rights. Even now, when "backlash" movements are prominent, these trends are continuing.

Despite the trends, public support for democratic values is still not secure. Stenner and Haidt (2018, p. 217) propose that authoritarianism is "something that sits just below the surface of any human society – including in the advanced liberal democracies at the heart of the Western world." Even in nations where almost everyone supports democracy in principle, many people do not accept or do not recognize the importance of the norms and institutions that democracy needs in order to function. A striking example of this gap is provided from a 1999 survey that asked people if they agreed or disagreed with the statement that "newspapers should be allowed to endorse or criticize political candidates": 36 percent disagreed, and 28 percent agreed, but not strongly. That is, despite a constitutional guarantee and two centuries of experience, only 35 percent strongly agreed with one of the most basic principles of a free press. Nevertheless, the potential pool of support for authoritarianism is declining, and this decline can be expected to continue.

Summary and Conclusions

Public confidence in government has declined in both Europe and the United States, and both have seen the appearance of "populist" movements that are critical of elites. In Europe, these movements have produced new political parties; in the United States, they have involved challenges within the parties. The causes of dissatisfaction, however, seem to be different. In Europe, dissatisfaction exists because some popular ideas are not represented among political elites. In the United States, the political system is more responsive to popular ideas, but ideological divergence between the parties has led to conflict and "gridlock." Several possible reasons for the growing ideological divergence in the United States are discussed.

Despite concerns about the recent rise of authoritarian movements, there is no evidence of a general decline in support for democracy. Public opinion continues to move in the direction of greater tolerance and support for the principle of equal rights. Therefore, the long-term movement toward democracy is likely to continue. The movement will not be steady or free of conflict, but it has deep roots in modern society.

References

AAPOR (American Association of Public Opinion Research). 2017. *An Evaluation of 2016 Election Polls in the U.S.* https://www.aapor.org/Education-Resources/Reports/An-Evaluation-of-2016-Election-Polls-in-the-U-S.aspx

Abramowitz, Alan I. and Steven Webster. 2016. "The Rise of Negative Partisanship and the Nationalization of US Elections in the 21st Century." *Electoral Studies* 41: 12–22.

Achen, Christopher H. and Larry M. Bartels. 2016. *Democracy for Realists.* Princeton, NJ: Princeton University Press.

Adams, James, Jane Green, and Caitlin Milazzo. 2012. "Has the British Public Depolarized Along With Political Elites? An American Perspective on British Public Opinion." *Comparative Political Studies* 45: 507–30.

Alesina, Alberto and Romain Wacziarg. 2000. "The Economics of Civic Trust." pp. 121–48 in *Disaffected Democracies*, eds Susan J. Pharr and Robert D. Putnam. Princeton, NJ: Princeton University Press.

Alexander, Jeffrey. 2019. "Frontlash/Backlash: The Crisis of Solidarity and the Threat to Civil Institutions." *Contemporary Sociology* 48: 5–11.

Alford, Robert. 1963. *Party and Society.* New York: Rand McNally.

Almond, Gabriel and Sidney Verba. 1963. *The Civic Culture.* Princeton, NJ: Princeton University Press.

American Political Science Association. 1950. *Toward a More Responsible Two-Party System.* New York: Rinehart & Co.

Anderson, Benedict. 2006. *Imagined Communities*, revised edition. London: Verso.

Anderson, Christopher J. and Jason D. Hecht. 2018. "The Preference for Europe: Public Opinion about European Integration Since 1952." *European Union Politics* 19: 617–38.

Axelrod, Robert. 1997. *The Complexity of Cooperation.* Princeton, NJ: Princeton University Press.

Baker, William D. and John R. Oneal. 2001. "Patriotism or Opinion Leadership?:

References

The Nature and Origins of the 'Rally 'Round the Flag' Effect." *Journal of Conflict Resolution* 45: 661–87.

Baldassarri, Delia and Andrew Gelman. 2008. "Partisans without Constraint: Political Polarization and Trends in American Public Opinion." *American Journal of Sociology* 114: 408–46.

Barry, Brian. 1990. "The Welfare State and the Relief of Poverty." *Ethics* 100: 503–29.

Bartels, Larry. 2003. "Democracy With Attitudes." pp. 48–82 in *Electoral Democracy*, eds George Rabinowitz and Michael B. MacKuen. Ann Arbor: University of Michigan Press.

Bartels, Larry. 2005. "Homer Gets a Tax Cut: Inequality and Public Policy in the American Mind." *Perspectives on Politics* 3, 15–31.

Bartels, Larry. 2008. *Unequal Democracy*. Princeton, NJ: Princeton University Press.

Bell, Daniel. 1962. *The End of Ideology*, revised edition. New York: Free Press.

Bell, Daniel. 1964. "The Dispossessed." pp. 1–46 in *The Radical Right*, ed. Daniel Bell. Garden City, NY: Doubleday.

Bell, Daniel. 1973. *The Coming of Post-Industrial Society*. New York: Basic Books.

Bell, Daniel. 1975. "Ethnicity and Social Change," in *Ethnicity: Theory and Experience*, eds Nathan Glazer and Daniel Patrick Moynihan. New York: Basic.

Berelson, Bernard R., Paul F. Lazarsfeld, and William N. McPhee. 1954. *Voting*. Chicago: University of Chicago Press.

Berinsky, Adam J. 2006. "American public opinion in the 1930s and 1940s: The analysis of quota-controlled sample survey data." *Public Opinion Quarterly* 70: 499–529.

Berinsky, Adam J., Eleanor Neff Powell, Eric Schickler, and Ian Brett Yohai. 2011. "Revisiting Public Opinion in the 1930s and 1940s." *PS: Political Science and Politics* 44: 515–20.

Berman, Nancy and Larry Bartels. 2014. "Mass Politics in Tough Times," pp. 1–39 in *Mass Politics in Tough Times*, eds Nancy Berman and Larry M. Bartels. Oxford: Oxford University Press.

Berning, Carl C. and Conrad Ziller. 2017. "Social trust and radical right-wing populist party preferences." *Acta Politica* 52: 198–217.

Bishop, Bill. 2009. *The Big Sort*. Boston: Houghton Mifflin.

Blumer, Herbert. 1990. *Industrialization as an Agent of Social Change*. New York: Aldine de Gruyter.

Bobo, Lawrence D. 2017. "Racism in Trump's America: Reflections on Culture, Sociology, and the 2106 Presidential Election." *British Journal of Sociology* S85–S104.

Borch, Casey B. 2007. *Whose Opinion Counts? An Analysis of the Opinion-Policy Linkage in the U. S. States*. Ph. D. dissertation, University of Connecticut.

References

Boxell, Levi, Matthew Gentzkow, and Jesse M. Shapiro. 2017. "Is the Internet Causing Political Polarization? Evidence from Demographics." NBER Working Paper 23258.

Brooks, Clem and Jeff Manza. 2008. *Why Welfare States Persist: The Importance of Public Opinion*. Chicago: University of Chicago Press.

Brooks, Clem, Paul Nieuwbeerta, and Jeff Manza. 2006. "Cleavage-Based Voting Behavior in Cross-National Perspective: Evidence from Six Postwar Democracies." *Social Science Research* 35: 88–128.

Butler, David E. and Donald E. Stokes. 1974. *Political Change in Britain*, revised edition. New York: St. Martin's.

Bourdieu, Pierre. 1979. "Public Opinion Does Not Exist." pp. 124–30 in *Communication and Class Struggle*, eds Armand Mattelart and Seth Siegelaub. New York: International General.

Campbell, Angus, Philip E. Converse, Warren F. Miller, and Donald E. Stokes. 1960. *The American Voter*. Chicago: University of Chicago Press.

Cantril, Hadley. 1951. *Public Opinion, 1935–46*. Princeton, NJ: Princeton University Press.

Card, David, Christian Dustmann, and Ian Preston. 2012. "Immigration, Wages, and Compositional Amenities." *Journal of the European Economic Association* 10: 78–119.

Carmines, Edward G. and James A. Stimson. 1989. *Issue Evolution: Race and the Transformation of American Politics*. Princeton, NJ: Princeton University Press.

Citrin, Jack and John Sides. 2008. "Immigration and the Imagined Community in Europe and the United States." *Political Studies* 56: 33–56.

Clark, Terry Nichols and Seymour Martin Lipset (eds). 2001. *The Breakdown of Class Politics*. Washington, DC: Woodrow Wilson Center Press.

Converse, Philip E. 1964. "The Nature of Belief Systems in Mass Publics." pp. 206–61 in *Ideology and Discontent*, ed. David E. Apter. Glencoe, IL: Free Press.

Converse, Philip E. 1975. "Public Opinion and Voting Behavior," in *Handbook of Political Science*, vol. 4, eds Fred I. Greenstein and Nelson W. Polsby. Reading, MA: Addison-Wesley.

Converse, Philip E. and Gregory B. Markus. 1979. "Plus ça change . . .: The New CPS Election Study Panel." *American Political Science Review* 73: 32–49.

Crone, Patricia. 1989. *Pre-Industrial Societies*. Oxford: Basil Blackwell.

Crutchfield, Robert D. and David Pettinicchio. 2009. " 'Cultures of Inequality': Ethnicity, Immigration, Social Welfare, and Imprisonment." *Annals of the American Academy of Political and Social Science* 623: 134–47.

Cubberley, Ellwood P. 1922. *A Brief History of Education*. Boston: Houghton Mifflin.

Dahrendorf, Ralf. 1959. *Class and Class Conflict in Industrial Society*. Stanford: Stanford University Press.

References

Dalton, Russell J. 2014. *Citizen Politics*, sixth edition. Los Angeles: Sage.

Davis, James A. 1980. "Conservative Weather in a Liberalizing Climate: Change in Selected NORC General Social Survey Items, 1972–1978." *Social Forces* 58: 1129–56.

De Ruggiero, Guido . 1927 [1959]. *The History of European Liberalism.* Boston: Beacon.

Dennison, James and Andrew Geddes. 2019. "A Rising Tide? The Salience of Immigration and the Rise of Anti-Immigration Political Parties in Western Europe." *Political Quarterly* 90: 107–16.

DeSilver, Drew. 2014. "How the most ideologically polarized Americans live different lives." https://www.pewresearch.org/fact-tank/2014/06/13/big-hou ses-art-museums-and-in-laws-how-the-most-ideologically-polarized-america ns-live-different-lives/

Desmet, Klaus and Romain Wacziarg. 2018. "The Cultural Divide." NBER Working Paper #24630.

Dicey, A. V. 1914. *Lectures on the Relation Between Law and Public Opinion in England.* London: Macmillan.

Dimaggio, Paul J., John Evans, and Bethany Bryson. 1996. "Have Americans' Social Attitudes Become More Polarized?" *American Journal of Sociology* 102: 690–755.

Douthat, Ross. 2017. "How Populism Stumbles." *New York Times* (February 1).

Downs, Anthony. 1957. *An Economic Theory of Democracy.* New York: Harper & Row.

Drezner, Daniel W. 2014. "The System Worked: Global Economic Governance During the Great Recession." *World Politics* 66: 123–64.

Durante, Ruben, Paolo Pinotti, and Andrea Tesei. 2019. "The Political Legacy of Entertainment TV." *American Economic Review* 109: 2497–530.

Eliasoph, Nina. 1998. *Avoiding Politics.* Cambridge: Cambridge University Press.

Ellis, Christopher and James A. Stimson. 2012. *Ideology in America.* New York: Cambridge University Press.

Ellis, Joseph J. 2018. *American Dialogue.* New York: Vintage.

Enns, Peter K., Paul M. Kellstedt, and Gregory E. McAvoy. 2012. "The Consequences of Partisanship in Economic Perceptions." *Public Opinion Quarterly* 76: 287–310.

Erikson, Robert S., Michael MacKuen, and James A. Stimson. 2002. *The Macro Polity.* New York: Cambridge University Press.

Evans, Geoffrey (ed.). 1999. *The End of Class Politics?* Oxford: Oxford University Press.

Eysenck, H. J. 1972. *Psychology is About People.* New York: Library Press.

Feinstein, Brian D. and Eric Schickler. 2008. "Platforms and Partners: The Civil Rights Realignment Reconsidered." *Studies in American Political Development* 22: 1–31.

References

Fetzer, Joel S. 2000. *Public Attitudes Toward Immigration in the United States, France, and Germany.* Cambridge: Cambridge University Press.

Fine, Gary Alan. 2006. "The Chaining of Social Problems: Solutions and Unintended Consequences in the Age of Betrayal." *Social Problems* 53: 3–26.

Fiorina, Morris P. and Samuel J. Abrams. 2008. "Political Polarization in the American Public." *Annual Review of Political Science* 11: 563–88.

Fischer, Claude S. 1978. "Urban-to-Rural Diffusion of Opinions in Contemporary America." *American Journal of Sociology* 84: 151–9.

Fischer, Claude S. 2010. *Made in America: A Social History of American Culture and Character.* Chicago: University of Chicago Press.

Fischer, Claude S. 2011. *Still Connected: Family and Friends in America Since 1970.* New York: Russell Sage.

Fischer, Claude S. 2017. "Explaining Trump." *Sociological Images* https://the societypages.org/socimages/2017/01/20/explaining-trump/

Fischer, David Hackett. 1991. *Albion's Seed: Four British Folkways in America.* New York: Oxford University Press.

Fishman, Noam and Alyssa Davis. 2017. "Americans Still See Big Government as Top Threat." https://news.gallup.com/poll/201629/americans-big-governm ent-top-threat.aspx

Foa, Roberto Stefan and Yascha Mounk. 2017. "The Signs of Deconsolidation." *Journal of Democracy* 28: 5–15.

Free, Lloyd A. and Hadley Cantril. 1967. *The Political Beliefs of Americans.* New Brunswick, NJ: Rutgers University Press.

Friedman, Benjamin M. 2005. *The Moral Consequences of Economic Growth.* New York: Random House.

Fukuyama, Francis. 2018. "Against Identity Politics." *Foreign Affairs* 97: 90–114.

Gallup. 2019a. "Immigration." https://news.gallup.com/poll/1660/immigration. aspx

Gallup. 2019b. "Labor Unions." https://news.gallup.com/poll/12751/labor-unio ns.aspx

Gallup, George. 1938. "Government and the Sampling Referendum." *Journal of the American Statistical Association* 33: 131–42.

Gamson, William A. and Andre Modigliani. 1989. "Media Discourse and Public Opinion on Nuclear Power: A Constructionist Approach." *American Journal of Sociology* 95: 1–37.

Geertz, Clifford. 1963. "The Integrative Revolution." pp. 105–57 in *Old Societies and New States*, ed. Clifford Geertz. New York: Free Press.

Gellner, Ernest. 1979. "The Social Roots of Egalitarianism." *Dialectics and Humanism* 4: 27–43.

Gelman, Andrew, David Park, Boris Shor, Joseph Bafumi, and Jeronimo Cortina. 2009. *Red State, Blue State, Rich State, Poor State.* Princeton, NJ: Princeton University Press.

References

Gentzkow, Matthew. 2016. "Polarization in 2016." Unpublished paper, Stanford University.

Gilens, Martin. 2012. *Affluence and Influence.* New York: Russell Sage Foundation and Princeton, NJ: Princeton University Press.

Glaeser, Edward L., Giacomo A. M. Ponzetto, and Andrei Shleifer. 2007. "Why Does Democracy Need Education?" *Journal of Economic Growth* 12: 77–99.

Goldthorpe, John H. 1987. *Social Mobility and Class Structure in Modern Britain.* Oxford: Oxford University Press.

Graetz, Michael and Ian Shapiro. 2006. *Death by A Thousand Cuts: The Fight Over Taxing Inherited Wealth.* Princeton, NJ: Princeton University Press.

Grusky, David B. and Jesper B. Sorensen. 1998. "Can Class Analysis be Salvaged?" *American Journal of Sociology* 103: 1187–234.

Guiso, Luigi, Paola Sapienza, and Luigi Zingales. 2016. "Monet's Error?" *Economic Policy* 31: 247–97.

Hanretty, Chris. 2016. "Here's Why Pollsters and Pundits Got Brexit Wrong." *Washington Post*, June 24.

Häusermann, Silja and Hanspeter Kriesi. 2015. "What do Voters Want?" pp. 202–30 in *The Politics of Advanced Capitalism*, eds Pablo Beramendi, Silja Häusermann, Herbert Kitschelt, and Hanspeter Kriesi, Cambridge: Cambridge University Press 2015.

Hayek, F. A. 1949. "The Intellectuals and Socialism." *University of Chicago Law Review* 16: 417–33.

Hechter, Michael. 2004. "From Class to Culture." *American Journal of Sociology* 110: 400–45.

Hetherington, Marc and Jonathan D. Weiler. 2009. *Authoritarianism and Polarization in American Politics.* New York: Cambridge University Press.

Hetherington, Marc and Jonathan D. Weiler. 2018. *Prius or Pickup?* Boston: Houghton Mifflin.

Hibbing, John R. and Elizabeth Theiss-Morse. 2002. *Stealth Democracy: Americans' Beliefs about How Government Should Work.* New York: Cambridge University Press.

Hillygus, D. Sunshine. 2016. "The Practice of Survey Research: Changes and Challenges." pp. 34–53 in *New Directions in Public Opinion Research*, second edition, ed. Adam Berinsky. New York: Routledge.

Hobolt, Sara B. 2016. "The Brexit Vote: A Divided Nation, a Divided Continent." *Journal of European Public Policy* 23: 1259–77.

Hobolt, Sara B., Thomas J. Leeper, and James Tilley. 2018. "Divided by the Vote: Affective Polarization in the Wake of Brexit." Unpublished paper.

Hofstadter, Richard. 1955. "The Pseudo-Conservative Revolt." pp. 75–96 in *The Radical Right*, ed. Daniel Bell. Garden City: Doubleday, 1964.

Hofstadter, Richard. 1962. "Pseudo-Conservatism Revisited: A Postscript." pp. 97–104 in *The Radical Right*, ed. Daniel Bell. Garden City: Doubleday, 1964.

References

House, James S. and William M. Mason. 1975. "Political Alienation in America, 1952–1968." *American Sociological Review* 40: 123–47.

Huckfeldt, Robert and John Sprague. 1988. "Choice, Social Structure, and Political Information: The Informational Coercion of Minorities." *American Journal of Political Science* 32: 467–82.

Hughes, Everett Cherrington. 1945. "Dilemmas and Contradictions of Status." *American Journal of Sociology* 50: 353–9.

Hyman, Herbert, and Charles R. Wright. 1979. *Education's Lasting Influence on Values*. Chicago: University of Chicago Press.

Hyman, Richard. 2010. "Trade Unions and 'Europe': Are the Members Out of Step?" *Relations Industrielles/Industrial Relations* 65: 3–29.

Inglehart, Ronald. 1977. *The Silent Revolution*. Princeton, NJ: Princeton University Press.

Inglehart, Ronald. 1990. *Culture Shift in Advance Industrial Society*. Princeton, NJ: Princeton University Press.

Inglehart, Ronald. 1997. *Modernization and Postmodernization*. Princeton, NJ: Princeton University Press.

Inglehart, Ronald and Pippa Norris. 2016. "Trump, Brexit, and the Rise of Populism: Economic Have-Nots and Cultural Backlash," HKS Working Paper RWP16–026.

Iyengar, Shanto, Guarav Sood, and Yphtac Lelkes. 2012. "Affect, Not Ideology: A Social Identity Perspective on Polarization." *Public Opinion Quarterly* 76: 405–31.

Jansen, Giedo, Geoffrey Evans, and Nan Dirk De Graaf. 2013. "Class Voting and Left–Right Party Positions: A Comparative Study of Fifteen Western Democracies, 1960–2005." pp. 46–86 in *Political Choice Matters*, eds Geoffrey Evans and Nan Dirk De Graaf. Oxford: Oxford University Press.

Jelen, Ted G. and Clyde Wilcox. 2003. "Causes and Consequences of Public Attitudes Toward Abortion: A Review and Research Agenda." *Public Opinion Quarterly* 56: 489–500.

Jennings, Will and Christopher Wlezien. 2018. "Election Polling Errors Across Time and Space." *Nature Human Behavior* 2: 276–83.

Kaufman, Jason and Matthew E. Kaliner. 2011. "The Re-Accomplishment of Place in Twentieth Century Vermont and New Hampshire." *Theory and Society* 40: 119–54.

Keeter, Scott Nick Hatley, Courtney Kennedy, and Arnold Lau. 2017. "What Low Response Rates Mean for Telephone Surveys." Pew Research Center. www.pewresearch.org.

Kerr, Clark and Abraham Siegel. 1954. "The Interindustry Propensity to Strike: An International Comparison," in *Industrial Conflict*, eds Arthur W. Kornhauser, Robert Dubin, and Arthur M. Ross. New York: McGraw-Hill.

Kersch, Ken I. 2014. "The Talking Cure: How Constitutional Argument Drives Constitutional Development." *Boston University Law Review* 94: 1083–108.

References

Key, V. O. 1961. *Public Opinion and American Democracy*. New York: Knopf.

Kinder, Donald R. and Nathan P. Kalmoe. 2017. *Neither Liberal nor Conservative: Ideological Innocence in the American Public*. Chicago: University of Chicago Press.

Kitschelt, Herbert P. and Rehm, Philipp. 2019. "Secular Partisan Realignment in the United States: The Socioeconomic Reconfiguration of White Partisan Support Since the New Deal Era." *Politics and Society* 47: 425–79.

Kluckhohn, Clyde. 1958. "Have there Been Discernible Shifts in American Values During the Last Generation?" pp. 145–217 in *The American Style*, ed. Elting E. Morison. New York: Harper & Brothers.

Kristol, Irving. 1995. *Neoconservatism: The Autobiography of an Idea*. New York: Free Press.

Krugman, Paul. 2019. "The Empty Quarters of U. S. Politics." *New York Times*, February 4.

Kuran, Timur. 1995. "The Inevitability of Future Revolutionary Surprises." *American Journal of Sociology* 100: 1528–51.

Kuziemko, Ilyana and Michael I. Norton. 2011. "The 'Last Place Aversion' Paradox." *Scientific American* (October 12).

Kuziemko, Ilyana, Michael Norton, Emmanuel Saez, and Stefanie Stantcheva. 2015. "How Elastic Are Preferences for Redistribution? Evidence from Randomized Survey Experiments." *American Economic Review* 105: 1478–508.

Kuziemko, Ilyana and Stefanie Stantcheva. 2013. "Our Feelings About Inequality: It's Complicated." *New York Times* (April 21).

Lakoff, George. 1996. *Moral Politics*. Chicago: University of Chicago Press.

Lazarsfeld, Paul F. 1944. "The Controversy over Detailed Interviews—An Offer For Negotiation." *Public Opinion Quarterly* 8: 38–60.

Lecky, W. E. H. 1877 [1920]. *History of European Morals*, new edition. London: Longmans, Green, and Co.

Lenz, Gabriel S. 2013. *Follow the Leader?* Chicago: University of Chicago Press.

Lerner, Daniel. 1958. *The Passing of Traditional Society*. Glencoe, IL: Free Press.

Lieber, Francis. 1839. *Manual of Political Ethics*, vol. 1. Philadelphia: Lippincott.

Lijphart, Arend. 1979. "Religious vs. Linguistic vs. Class Voting: The 'Crucial Experiment' of Comparing Belgium, Canada, South Africa, and Switzerland." *American Political Science Review* 73: 442–58.

Lipset, Seymour Martin. 1960. *Political Man*. New York: Doubleday.

Lipset, Seymour Martin. 1962. "A Changing American Character?" In *Culture and Social Character*, eds Seymour Martin Lipset and Leo Lowenthal. New York: Free Press.

Lipset, Seymour Martin. 1964. "Beyond the Backlash." *Encounter* 83: 11–24.

Lipset, Seymour Martin. 1970. *Revolution and Counter-Revolution*, revised edition. Garden City, NY: Anchor.

References

Lipset, Seymour Martin. 1981. *Political Man,* expanded edition. Baltimore, MD: Johns Hopkins University Press.

Lipset, Seymour Martin and Earl Raab. 1970. *The Politics of Unreason.* New York: Harper & Row.

Lukes, Steven. 2003. "Epilogue: The Grand Dichotomy of the Twentieth Century." pp. 602–26 in *The Cambridge History of Twentieth Century Political Thought,* eds Terence Ball and Richard Bellamy. Cambridge: Cambridge University Press.

Luks, Samantha and Michael Salamone. 2008. "Abortion." pp. 80–107 in *Public Opinion and Constitutional Controversy,* eds Nathaniel Persily, Jack Citrin, and Patrick J. Egan. New York: Oxford University Press.

Luttmer, Erzo F. P. 2001. "Group Loyalty and the Taste for Redistribution." *Journal of Political Economy* 109: 500–28.

McCall, Leslie and Lane Kenworthy. 2009. "Americans' Social Policy Preferences in the Era of Rising Inequality." *Perspectives on Politics* 7: 459–84.

Mackinac Center. 2019. "The Overton Window." https://www.mackinac.org/OvertonWindow.

McPherson, Miller, Lynn Smith-Lovin, and James M. Cook. 2001. "Birds of a Feather: Homophily in Social Networks." *Annual Review of Sociology* 27: 415–44.

MacRae, Duncan Jr. 1967. *Parliament, Parties, and Society in France, 1946–1958.* New York: St. Martin's.

Mair, Peter. 2007. "Left–Right Orientations," in *The Oxford Handbook of Political Behavior,* eds Russell J. Dalton and Hans-Dieter Klingemann. Oxford: Oxford University Press.

Mair, Peter. 2013. *Ruling the Void: The Hollowing of Western Democracy.* London: Verso.

Manza, Jeff and Clem Brooks. 1999. *Social Cleavages and Political Change.* Oxford: Oxford University Press.

Manza, Jeff and Clem Brooks. 2012. "How Sociology Lost Public Opinion: A Genealogy of a Missing Concept in the Study of the Political." *Sociological Theory* 30: 89–113.

Marx, Karl. 1852 [1969]. "The Eighteenth Brumaire of Louis Bonaparte." pp. 394–487 in Karl Marx and Frederick Engels, *Selected Works,* vol. 1. Moscow: Progress Publishers.

Meltzer, Allan H. and Scott F. Richard. 1981. "A Rational Theory of the Size of Government." *Journal of Political Economy* 89: 914–27.

Michels, Robert. 1915. *Political Parties,* translated by Eden and Cedar Paul. New York: Hearst's International Library.

Milne, R. S. and H. C. McKenzie. 1959. *Marginal Seat, 1955.* London: Hansard Society.

Mirowsky, John and Ross, Catherine E. 1998. "Education, Personal Control, Lifestyle, and Health." *Research on Aging* 20: 415–49.

References

Molloy, Raven, Christopher L. Smith, and Abigail K. Wozniak. 2011. "Internal Migration in the United States." NBER Working Paper 17307.

Mueller, John E. 1973. *War, Presidents, and Public Opinion*. New York: Wiley.

Murray, Charles. 2012. *Coming Apart*. New York: Crown Forum.

Mutz, Diana C. 2018. "Status Threat, Not Economic Hardship, Explains the 2016 Presidential Vote." *PNAS* 115: E4330–E4339.

Myrdal, Gunnar. 1960. *Beyond the Welfare State*. New Haven, CT: Yale University Press.

Newport, Frank. 2016. "Americans Still Say Upper-Income Pay too Little in Taxes." https://news.gallup.com/poll/190775/americans-say-upper-income-pay-little-taxes.aspx

Nisbet, Robert. 1975. "Public Opinion versus Popular Opinion." *The Public Interest* 41.

Norton, Michael I. and Dan Ariely. 2011. "Building a Better America: One Wealth Quintile at a Time." *Perspectives on Psychological Science* 6: 9–12.

Oliver, J. Eric and Wendy M. Rahn. 2016. "Rise of the Trumpenvolk: Populism in the 2016 Election." *Annals of the American Academy of Political and Social Science* 667: 189–206.

Page, Benjamin I. and Robert Y. Shapiro. 1992. *The Rational Public*. Chicago: University of Chicago Press.

Pascarella, Ernest T. and Terenzini, Patrick T. 1991. *How College Affects Students*. San Francisco: Jossey-Bass.

Persily, Nathaniel. 2008. "Introduction." pp. 3–16 in *Public Opinion and Constitutional Controversy*, eds Nathaniel Persily, Jack Citrin, and Patrick J. Egan. New York: Oxford University Press.

Pew Research Center. 2014. "Political Polarization in the American Public." http://www.people-press.org/2014/06/12/political-polarization-in-the-american-public/

Pharr, Susan J. and Robert D. Putnam (eds). 2000. *Disaffected Democracies*. Princeton, NJ: Princeton University Press.

Piketty, Thomas. 2018. "Brahmin Left vs Merchant Right: Rising Inequality and the Changing Structure of Political Conflict." WID.world Working Paper 2018/7.

Pinker, Steven. 2011. *The Better Angels of Our Nature*. New York: Penguin.

Plamenatz, John. 1975. "Public Opinion and Political Consciousness." *Political Studies* 29: 342–51.

Policy Agendas Project. 2015. *Policy Moods Codebook*. https://www.comparativeagendas.net/us

Pratto, Felicia, Jim Sidanius, Lisa M. Stallworth, and Bertram F. Malle. 1994. "Social Dominance Orientation: A Personality Variable Predicting Social and Political Attitudes." *Journal of Personality and Social Psychology* 67: 741–63.

Putnam, Robert. 1993. *Making Democracy Work: Civic Traditions in Modern Italy*. Princeton, NJ: Princeton University Press.

References

Putnam, Robert. 2000. *Bowling Alone: The Collapse and Revival of American Community*. New York: Simon and Schuster.

RealClear Politics. 2016. "General Election: Trump versus Clinton." https://www.realclearpolitics.com/epolls/2016/president/us/general_election_trump_vs_clinton-5491.html

Rodrik, Dani. 2011. *The Globalization Paradox*. Oxford: Oxford University Press.

Rokkan, Stein. 1961. "Mass Suffrage, Secret Voting and Political Participation." *European Journal of Sociology* 2: 132–52.

Rose, Richard and Ian McAllister. 1986. *Voters Begin to Choose: From Closed-Class to Open Elections in Britain*. London: Sage.

Runciman, W. G. 1966. *Relative Deprivation and Social Justice*. London: Routledge.

Russell, John. 1823. *An Essay on the History of the English Government and Constitution*. London: Longman, Green, Longman, Roberts, & Green.

Rydgren, Jens. 2009. "Social Isolation? Social Capital and Radical Right-wing Voting in Western Europe." *Journal of Civil Society* 5: 129–50.

Sasse, Ben. 2018. *Them: Why We Hate Each Other – And How to Heal*. New York: St. Martin's.

Schlesinger, Arthur M., Jr. 1962. "A Humanist Looks at Empirical Social Research." *American Sociological Review* 27: 768–71.

Schlozman, Kay Lehman and Sidney Verba. 1979. *Injury to Insult: Unemployment, Class, and Political Response*. Cambridge, MA: Harvard University Press.

Schuman, Howard and Stanley Presser. 1981. *Questions and Answers in Attitude Surveys*. New York: Academic Press.

Sears, David O., John J. Hetts, Jim Sidanius, and Lawrence Bobo. 2000. "Race in American Politics: Framing the Debates." pp. 1–43 in *Racialized Politics*, eds David O. Sears, Jim Sidanius, and Lawrence Bobo. Chicago: University of Chicago Press.

Sears, David O., Jim Sidanius, and Lawrence Bobo (eds). 2000. *Racialized Politics*. Chicago: University of Chicago Press.

Shapiro, Robert Y. and Yaeli Bloch-Elkon. 2006. "Political Polarization and the Rational Public." Paper presented at the annual conference of the American Association for Public Opinion Research.

Shapiro, Robert Y. and Yaeli Bloch-Elkon. 2008. "Do the Facts Speak for Themselves? Partisan Disagreement as a Challenge to Democratic Competence." *Critical Review* 20: 115–39.

Singer, Peter. 1981. *The Expanding Circle*. New York: Farrar, Straus, & Giroux.

Skocpol, Theda. 1996. *Boomerang: Clinton's Health Security Effort and the Turn Against Government in U.S. Politics*. New York: Norton.

Smith, Tom W. 1987. "That Which We Call Welfare By Any Other Name Would Smell Sweeter: An Analysis of the Impact of Question Wording On Response Patterns." *Public Opinion Quarterly* 51: 75–83.

References

Smith, Tom W. 1990. "Liberal and Conservative Trends in the United States Since World War II." *Public Opinion Quarterly* 54: 479–507.

Soroka, Stuart N. and Christopher Wlezien. 2010. *Degrees of Democracy: Politics, Public Opinion, and Policy.* New York: Cambridge University Press.

Stenner, Karen and Jonathan Haidt. 2018. "Authoritarianism is not a Momentary Madness, but an Eternal Dynamic Within Liberal Democracies." pp. 175–220 in *Can It Happen Here?*, ed. Cass R. Sunstein. New York: Dey St.

Stigler, George A. 1970. "Director's Law of Public Income Redistribution." *Journal of Law and Economics* 13: 1–10.

Stille, Alexander. 2006. *The Sack of Rome.* New York: Penguin.

Stimson, James A. 1991. *Public Opinion in America: Moods, Cycles, and Swings.* Boulder, CO: Westview.

Stinchcombe, Arthur. 1989. "Education, Exploitation, and Class Consciousness." pp. 168–72 in Erik Olin Wright et al., *The Debate on Classes.* London: Verso.

Stouffer, Samuel A. 1955. *Communism, Conformity, and Civil Liberties.* New York: Doubleday.

Sullivan, Andrew. 2018. "America's New Religions." *New York* (December 7).

Svallfors, Stefan. 2005. "Class and Conformism: A Comparison of Four Western Countries." *European Societies* 7: 255–86.

Thornton, Arland. 2001. "The Developmental Paradigm, Reading History Sideways, and Family Change." *Demography* 38: 449–65.

Tilly, Charles. 1983. "Speaking Your Mind without Elections, Surveys, or Social Movements." *Public Opinion Quarterly* 47: 461–78.

Tocqueville, Alexis de. 1850 [1969]. *Democracy in America*, translated by J. P. Mayer. Garden City, NY: Anchor.

Touraine, Alain. 1971. *The Post-Industrial Society.* New York: Random House.

Traugott, Michael W. 2005 "The Accuracy of the National Preelection Polls in the 2004 Presidential Election." *Public Opinion Quarterly* 69: 642–54.

van der Waal, Jeroen, Peter Achterberg, and Dick Houtman. 2007. "Class Is Not Dead – It Has Been Buried Alive: Class Voting and Cultural Voting in Postwar Western Societies (1956–1990)." *Politics and Society* 35: 403–26.

Weakliem, David L. 2002. "The Effects of Education on Political Opinions: An International Study." *International Journal of Public Opinion Research* 14: 141–57.

Weakliem, David L. 2010–2019. Just the Social Facts, Ma'am (blog) https://justthesocialfacts.blogspot.com

Weakliem, David L. 2013. "The United States: Still the Politics of Diversity." pp. 114–36 in *Political Choice Matters*, eds Geoffrey Evans and Nan Dirk De Graaf. Oxford: Oxford University Press.

Weakliem, David L. 2015. "Mobility, Measuring the Effects of." *Blackwell Encyclopedia of Sociology*, second edition. Malden, MA: Blackwell.

Weakliem, David L. 2016. "More people think abortion should always be legal.

References

And more people think it should never be legal." *Washington Post*, February 19.

Weakliem, David L. and Julia P. Adams. 2011. "What Do We Mean by 'Class Politics'?" *Politics and Society* 39: 475–96.

Weakliem, David L., Robert Andersen, and Anthony F. Heath. 2005. "By Popular Demand: The Effect of Public Opinion on Income Inequality." *Comparative Sociology* 4: 260–84.

Weakliem, David L. and Robert Biggert. 1999. "Region and Political Opinion in the Contemporary United States." *Social Forces* 77: 863–86.

Weakliem, David L. and Robert Biggert. 2013. "Not Asking for Much: Public Opinion and Redistribution from the Rich." *Comparative Sociology* 12: 66–94.

Wetts, Rachel and Robb Willer. 2018. "Privilege on the Precipice: Perceived Racial Status Threats Lead White Americans to Oppose Welfare Programs." *Social Forces* 97: 793-822.

Wilson, James Q. 1993. *The Moral Sense*. New York: Free Press.

Wilson, James Q. 1995. *Political Organizations*. Princeton, NJ: Princeton University Press.

Wirth, Louis. 1938. "Urbanism as a Way of Life." *American Journal of Sociology* 44: 1–24.

Wilkinson, Richard G. and Kate G. Pickett. 2017. "The Enemy Between Us: The Psychological and Social Costs of Inequality." *European Journal of Social Psychology* 47: 11–24.

Wlezien, Christopher. 1995. "The Public as Thermostat: Dynamics of Preferences for Spending." *American Journal of Political Science* 39: 981–1000.

Woodward, C. Vann. 1959. "The Populist Heritage and the Intellectual." *The American Scholar* 29: 55–72.

Yglesias, Matt. 2019. "The Great Awokening." *Vox*. https://www.vox.com/2019/3/22/18259865/great-awokening-white-liberals-race-polling-trump-2020

Zakaria, Fareed. 2017. "The Country is Frighteningly Polarized. This is Why." *Washington Post* (June 15).

Zaller, John. 1992. *The Nature and Origins of Mass Opinion*. New York: Cambridge University Press.

Zaller, John. 2003. "Coming to Grips with V. O. Key's Concept of Latent Opinion." In *Electoral Democracy*, eds Michael MacKuen and George Rabinowitz. Ann Arbor: University of Michigan Press.

Zaller, John. 2012. "What *Nature and Origins* Leaves Out." *Critical Review* 24: 569–642.

Znaniecki, Florian. 1952. *Modern Nationalities*. Urbana: University of Illinois Press.

174

Index

175

Index

Bobo, Lawrence D. 99
Borch, Casey B. 11
Bourdieu, Pierre 15, 16
Boxell, Levi 64, 70
Britain 5, 38, 148
    competitive elections 37–8
    Conservative governments 88, 89
    economic development 126
    ethnic and religious tolerance 128
    party support 45, 67; class differences in
        37
    referendum on EU membership (2016) 9
    social changes 70
Brooks, Clem 6, 11, 21, 47
Brown, Michael 100
Bush, George W. 92, 95, 96
Butler, David E. 55

California 56, 132
Campbell, Angus 73
Canada 5
    see also Montreal; Toronto
Cantril, Hadley 55–6, 84
Carmines, Edward G. 49
Catholics
    Protestants and 28, 128; differences
        between 31, 46
    regional differences in variety of
        opinions 35
    white 33, 34
Change 15–17, 111, 115
    aggregate 85–7
    individual 16, 83
    long-term 118–35
    negative, profound 154
    short-term 83–117
    triggered 112
    uneven pace of 110
    see also social change
Citrin, Jack 133, 149
civil liberties
    differences over 148
    support for 47, 56–7, 118, 125, 130,
        147
civil rights 76, 81
    peaceful march attacked by police 112
    people opposed to 109
Civil Rights Act (US 1964) 34, 79, 108,
    111
civil rights movement 28
    goals of 113
Clark, Terry Nichols 44
class

effects on voting choices/changes in
    patterns 6, 43–8
industrialization and the rise of 37–9
see also social class
class differences 26, 36
    decline in/of 40, 41–2
    equally large among all ethnic groups 35
    material interests especially relevant to
        30
    opinion on economic issues 39
    party support 43–4
    reduced 37
class divisions 36
    decline of 41
    new, rise of 42–3
Clinton, Bill 87
Clinton, Hillary 9, 145
coalitions 80, 132, 147
    loose 63, 149
Communists 13, 15, 74t, 78, 104–5, 147
    conservative position on 74, 75
constitutional matters see US Constitution
contemporary politics 68, 81, 144
    differences hard to explain in terms of
        33
Converse, Philip E. 55, 59, 73, 83
crime 56, 85–6, 94, 103–4
    issues related to 106
    reducing poverty would reduce 32
    tough policies promised against 108
Crutchfield, Robert D. 11
Cubberley, Ellwood P. 128

Danish People's Party 141
De Graaf, Nan Dirk 44
De Ruggiero, Guido 132
death penalty 15, 29, 32
    abolished 13, 128
    support for 13, 56, 83, 85f, 86, 103;
        changes in 93; decline in 104
democracy 1, 37, 121
    future of 2; question about 155
    modernization and support for 124, 125
    surveys as way to improve the operation
        of 4
    views of 127
    see also liberal democracy; participatory
        democracy; representative democracy
Dennison, James 109
Desmet, Klaus 69, 70
Dicey, A. V. 31
divorce 84, 125
    greater frequency of 47

176

Index

Index

Index

Index

internationalism 47
Italy 137, 148, 156
  differences among regions 30
  women's support to conservative parties 46
  see also Five Star Movement
Iyengar, Shanto 65, 67

Jansen, Giedo 44
Jelen, Ted G. 130–1
Jennings, Will 9
Jews 33, 128
Johnson, Lyndon 34, 108

Kaliner, Matthew E. 32
Kalmoe, Nathan P. 81
Kaufman, Jason 32
Kellstedt, Paul M. 96
Kerr, Clark 41
Kersch, Ken I. 154
Key, V. O. 1, 16, 47
Kinder, Donald R. 81
Kitschelt, Herbert P. 48, 50, 73
Kluckhohn, Clyde 111, 129, 135
Korean War (1950–3) 13, 15
Kriesi, Hanspeter 72, 73, 80, 123
Kristol, Irving 154
Krugman, Paul 80
Kuziemko, Ilyana 88, 90, 93

labor parties 39
labor unions 39, 59, 102
  attitudes to 71
  decline in support for 16
  opinions about 5, 88
Lakoff, George 80
Lazarsfeld, Paul F. 21, 23–4, 25, 34, 51, 71, 72, 76, 78, 150
League of Nations 84
Lecky, W. E. H. 132
Leeper, Thomas J. 67
legal abortion 63*f*
  correlations with opinions on 64
  support for 101, 114
Lelkes, Yphtac 65, 67
Lerner, Daniel 130
lesbians *see* gays and lesbians
less-educated people 54, 121, 122, 143
  opinions of 119
liberal democracy 121, 136–61
liberal trends 106–8, 119, 130–1
Lieber, Francis 2
Lipset, Seymour Martin 19–20, 21, 29–30,

35–6, 37, 44, 79, 95, 108, 109, 120–1, 144, 152
low-wage workers 1
lower classes 38, 51, 80
  divided 90
  pressure to respond to opinions of 131
  prevailing opinion in 39
lower-income groups 29–30
Luttmer, Erzo F. P. 122

MacKuen, Michael 11, 86
MacRae, Duncan 35
Maine 138
Mair, Peter 54, 58, 136, 138
Manza, Jeff 6, 11, 21, 47
marginalized groups 42, 79
Markus, Gregory B. 83
marriage
  later 47
  laws against 97
  sex relations before 101–2
  see also same-sex marriage
Marx, Karl 38
McAllister, Ian 40–1
McAvoy, Gregory E. 96
McKenzie, H. C. 33
McPhee, William N. 21, 23–4, 25, 34, 51, 71, 72, 76, 78, 150
Mexico 124
Michels, Robert 70
middle class 29, 38, 39, 41
  concern with the interests of 33
  educated 147
  expansion of 3
  occupations of 35–6
  political differences between working class and 47
  programs that help 91
  support for parties of the left 37
Middle East 46
Milazzo, Caitlin 67, 70
Miller, Warren F. 73
Milne, R. S. 33
minimum wage 1, 13–14, 15, 102
  increasing 62, 71; majority support for 56
Minnesota 138
minorities 35–6
  committed 151
  informational coercion of 24
  see also ethnic minorities; racial minorities; religious minorities
modernization 118

180

Index

economic opinions and 131
nationalism and 132–4
public opinion and 123–31, 135
Modigliani. Andre 115
Montreal 132
more-educated people 120–1, 122, 134
 liberalism 75, 118–19
 now more likely to support parties of the
  left 76
 tolerance and internationalism 47
Mounk, Yascha 156
Muslims 46, 57
Mutz, Diana C. 78, 143
Myrdal, Gunnar 132

National Rally (French "new right" party)
 141
nationalism 132–4
nativists 144
Nazi Germany 126
neoliberalism 149
Netherlands 145
New Hampshire 32
New York (State & City) 29
Nieuwbeerta, Paul 6
Nigeria 124
Nixon, Richard 108–9, 152
Norris, Pippa 109
Norton, Michael 88, 90, 92, 93

Obama, Barack 87, 95, 139, 146, 152, 153
Occupy Wall Street movement 90
originalism 153–5
Page, Benjamin I. 86, 93
parallel publics 93–5
 example of 94f
participatory democracy 158–9
particularism 72–3
party images 33, 58
Perot, Ross 138, 158
Persily, Nathaniel 17
Pettinicchio, David 11
Pew Research Cemter 32, 59, 64, 100
Pharr, Susan J. 136
Piketty, Thomas 45, 46
Pinker, Steven 128, 130, 135
Pinotti, Paolo 145–6
Plamenatz, John 2
polarization
 changes in 62–7
 consequences of 60–2
 definitions of 59–60
 ideological 96

partisan 151, 152
 rise in 144; explanations of 67–9;
  research on 69–71
 see also political polarization
Policy Agendas Project 106, 107
political movements 109, 142
 activity of 78
political polarization 22, 69
 increased 59–60, 68, 82, 96, 158
politics 25, 32, 39, 47, 77, 80–1, 136, 143,
 150, 151, 159
 activity in 59
 attention to 34; poor people and 30
 backlash in 108, 109
 cultural 72
 cynicism about 146
 democratic 70
 discussion of 17–18; popular 24;
  restricting 67
 electoral 79
 ethnicity, region and religion in 37
 group differences in 40
 identity 22
 illiberal 69
 interest 72
 involvement in 145; lower classes 38
 local 144
 military tradition of staying out of 158
 national 155
 populist movements' contribution to 142
 post-truth 95
 status 72, 76
 see also contemporary politics
poor people 51, 77, 143, 159
 assistance/aid to 114, 115, 128;
  government 88
 government has responsibility to help 58
 little attention to politics 30
 party closely associated with 39
 programs that help: spending on 32;
  turning against 90
 rich and: gap increased between 90;
  income differences between rich and
  48, 86
 standard of living of 30
 urban 38
 willingness to help 91
 working 115
popular opinion 20
 see also unpopular opinions
populism 141–2
 response to 146–7
 sources of: political 142–3; social 143–4

Index

Index

Index